Signature Cocktails & Appetizers *from* Around the World

Volume II
in
Linda Lang's Taste of Travel Series

By
Linda Lang

All Rights Reserved
Copyright ©2015
Linda Lang's Taste of Travel

*Dedicated to All Those
Who Celebrate the
Best in Life,
Best in Travel,
Best in Pleasure for the Palate,
and the
Talented Mixologists, Chefs,
Magnificent Hotels and Cruise Lines
That Make It All Possible.*

Acknowledgements

A big thank you goes to all the hotels and cruise lines who so graciously shared their cocktail and appetizer recipes with us. Without the creative contributions of the talented mixologists and chefs around the world who strive daily to take the enjoyment of both cocktails and appetizers to new heights, our pleasures would be lacking.

To all who helped assemble the information required to create this book—Madelyn Alster, Ann-Rebecca Laschever, Arnelle Kendall, Barbara Czelusniak, Carolin Meltendorf, Christina McGoldrick, Emanuela Apicella, Gonca Dietrich, Chloe Hager, Janine Cifelli, Jeime Bjordal, Joshua Preston, Kayla Louttit, Lauren Swoboda, Christina Le, Mark Liebermann, Martha Morano, Megan Sterritt, Nestor Lana, Baeza, Rebecka Norman, Richard Rooney, Ross Belfer, Shae Geary, Shari Mycek, Sharon Rooney, Stephanie Norby, Susah Chou, Suzanne Flores, Tracey Brumback, Vincent Pauchon and all the others who helped make this book possible — a big thank you to each and every one. Finally, to Krysten Johnson, whose creativity and patience are unsurpassed, and my good friends Jan Juhl, Maggie Rogers and Sonia Howard, your unfailing encouragement and support will always be deeply appreciated.

Cover and Interior Design:
Krysten Johnson, KJ Design, KJDesign4u@aol.com

Editor:
Sonia Howard

Photo Credits
Front Cover Photo: Toucan Hill

Back Cover Photos (*top to bottom*):
The Milestone Hotel, El Conquistador Resort, Blantyre, Grand Velas Riviera Nayarit, Laucala Island

Section Title Page Photos provided by:
Metropolitan: Chandler's at Cape Rey, *In the Countryside:* Linda Lang, *In the Islands:* Laucala Island
South of the Border: Velas Vallarta, *Afloat:* Uniworld Boutique River Cruise Collection
Appetizers: Jade Mountain, *Cocktail Essentials:* Linda Lang, *Appetizer Essentials:* Linda Lang

Property and Recipe Photo Credits
Aqua Expeditions, Tower at lebua, Beau Rivage, bbar, Blantyre, The BodyHoliday, Brown TLV Urban Hotel, The Bungalow, Casa Velas, Chandler's at Cape Rey, Condado Plaza Hilton, El Conquistador Resort, The Four Seasons Safari Lodge, Grand Velas Riviera Maya, Grand Velas Riviera Nayarit, The Greenbrier, The Greenwich Hotel, Hacienda Petac, Hamanasi Adventure and Dive Resort, Hotel Hassler Roma, Hotel Casa 425, Jade Mountain, The Lafayette Hotel, Laucala Island, Hôtel Le Toiny, Tower Club at lebua, Matlali Hotel, The Milestone Hotel, Montague on the Gardens, The Oyster Box, Palazzo Avino, QT Sydney, Regent Berlin, Royal Blues Hotel, The Rubens at the Palace, Scrub Island Resort, Singular Patagonia, South Seas Island Resort, Tenaya Lodge, Toucan Hill, Uniworld Boutique River Cruise Collection, Velas Vallarta, W Scottsdale, and Wharekauhau.

Foreword

The delights of the palate may change over time but they seldom lessen. As our travels increase and our experiences widen, we continue to discover new tastes and pleasures. One enjoyment many of us share is the art of mixology and sampling its creations.

Open your mind, take a deep breath and fully experience the adventure that awaits you on every page of this book. You'll find not only interesting twists on old favorites but totally unique cocktail recipes to try with friends. You'll also read stories, learn about and see beautiful photos of the magnificent hotels, resorts and river cruise lines around the globe that serve these specialties and have shared their recipes with us.

And what better complements an enjoyable cocktail hour than a selection of interesting, savory appetizers? Following the section presenting our cocktail recipes is a second section filled with a wide variety of delectable appetizers to accompany your cocktail of choice. Lobster, crab, tacos, shrimp, calamari, chicken, blackened bluefin tuna, shrimp bruschetta, trout ceviche, tequila grilled shrimp shooters -- check them out for yourselves. The recipes and photos are all there.

OTHER BOOKS BY LINDA LANG:

FIVE STAR RECIPES *from* WORLD FAMOUS HOTELS & RESORTS
Volume I in Linda Lang's Taste of Travel Series

THE PARTY PLANNER (eBook)

FAVORITE PARTY RECIPES (eBook)

Copyright © 2015, Linda Lang's Taste of Travel
All rights reserved.
Printed by CreateSpace, an Amazon Company

While every effort has been taken to present correctly and completely the cocktail and appetizer recipes provided by the contributing properties/river cruise lines, their mixologists and chefs, Linda Lang, Author, and Linda Lang's Taste of Travel, Publisher, do not guarantee 100% accuracy of the information provided. The Author and Publisher do not accept responsibility for any errors, omissions or inaccuracies or for any liability or loss incurred from use the information provided herein.

All text, images, and other materials within this book are subject to the copyright and other intellectual property rights of the Publisher except where specifically credited to the original providers. These materials may not be reproduced, distributed, modified, transmitted electronically, or otherwise copied or utilized without the express written permission of the Publisher and original providers. Links to suggested websites containing additional data are for informational purposes only and are not endorsements or guarantees of any kind whatsoever.

Contents

Acknowledgements — 6

Foreword — 7

Introduction — 15

Cocktails in Metropolitan Locales

Tower Club at lebua — 18
   Tropical Bliss — 19

Beau-Rivage Palace — 20
   City Lights — 21

QT Sydney — 22
   Barrel-Aged Rendezvous — 23

The Milestone Hotel — 24
   The Milestone Old Fashioned — 25

Hotel Hassler Roma — 26
   Veruschka Cocktail — 27

Hotel Casa 425 — 28
   Very Berry Spicy Margarita — 29

Regent Berlin — 30
   Espressotini — 31

Montague on the Gardens — 32
   Thyme Sloes Down — 33

bbar — 34
   Bushman's Delight — 35

The Lafayette Hotel — 36
   The Smoking Red Rose — 37

Brown TLV Urban Hotel — 38
    Orient Express — 39

The Greenwich Hotel — 40
    Agri Cola — 41

Royal Blues Hotel — 42
    Fluffy Bunny Cocktail — 43

The Rubens — 44
    Rubens Royal Blush — 45

W Scottsdale Hotel — 46
    Vitamin W Cocktail — 47

The Bungalow — 48
    Bitchin' Sangria — 49

Chandler's Bar & Lounge at Cape Rey — 50
    Beet Infused Rosemary Ginger Cocktail — 51

Cocktails in the Countryside

Palazzo Avino — 54
    Sunlight Martini — 55

The Greenbrier — 56
    The Greenbrier's Original Mint Julep — 57

Blantyre — 58
    Gilded Age Cocktail — 59

Wharekauhau Lodge — 60
    The Perfect Wharekauhau Gin Martini — 61

The Oyster Box — 62
    Umhlanga Schling — 63

Tenaya Lodge at Yosemite — 64
    High Sierra Bloody Mary — 65

Four Seasons Safari Lodge — 66
   Smashing Pumpkins — 67

Cocktails in the Islands

Toucan Hill — 70
   Caribbean Pink Passion — 71

Condado Plaza Hilton — 72
   Mojito Caribe Frozen — 73

Hôtel Le Toiny — 74
   Cobana Cocktail — 75

Scrub Island Resort, Spa & Marina — 76
   Scrub Island Flirt — 77

South Seas Island Resort — 78
   Captiva Cooler — 79

Laucala Island — 80
   Laucala Lagoon — 81

Jade Mountain — 82
   Stairway to Heaven — 83

The BodyHoliday — 84
   Lemon Rose Cocktail — 85

Cocktails South of the Border

El Conquistador Resort & Las Casitas Village — 88
   Sangria de Coco — 89

Hacienda Petac — 90
   El Flamboyan — 91

Velas Vallarta — 92
   Cucumber & Habanero Chili Margarita — 93

Grand Velas Riviera Maya	*94*
Mango Caribe	*95*
Matlali Hotel	*96*
Macho Margarita	*97*
Casa Velas	*98*
Passion Fruit Dry Martini	*99*
Hamanasi Adventure & Dive Resort	*100*
Coco Rumba	*101*
Grand Velas Riviera Nayarit	*102*
Basil Martini	*103*
The Singular Patagonia	*104*
Rhubarb Sour	*105*

Cocktails Afloat

Aqua Expeditions' Aqua Mekong	*108*
Kampot Fix	*109*
Uniworld Boutique River Cruise Collection	*110*
Zorro Dry Martini	*111*

Appetizers

The BodyHoliday	*114*
Lemon Grass Shrimp Skewers	*115*
Casa Velas	*116*
"Emiliano" Tuna with Avocado Aguachile	*117*
Condado Plaza Hilton	*118*
Tequila Grilled Shrimp Shooter	*119*
El Conquistador Resort	*120*
Salmorejo de Jueyes	*121*

Grand Velas Riviera Maya	*122*
Breaded Mussels	*123*
The Greenwich Hotel	*124*
Locanda Verde's Crab Crostino	*125*
Hotel Casa 425	*126*
Esquites (Roasted Corn Dip)	*127*
The Lafayette Hotel Swim Club & Bungalows	*128*
Pacific Bay Scallop Bruschetta	*129*
Laucala Island	*130*
Coral Trout Ceviche	*131*
Hôtel Le Toiny	*132*
Carpaccio and Ceviche of Mahi-Mahi	*133*
Tower Club at lebua	*134*
Seafood Taco	*135*
Matlali Hotel	*136*
Shrimp Ceviche	*137*
The Oyster Box	*138*
Pimm's Cured Salmon	*139*
Palazzo Avino	*140*
King Lobster on Bread "Pizzaiola" Style	*141*
Velas Vallarta	*142*
Seafood Bruschetta	*143*
Royal Blues Hotel	*144*
Diver Scallops with Carnaroli Risotto (Dairy Free)	*145*
Toucan Hill	*146*
Curry Coconut Shrimp with Pineapple & Carmelized Leeks	*147*
Jade Mountain	*148*
Spicy Calamari with Fresh Ginger	*149*

QT Sydney   *150*
   Bringing Back the "Vol-au-Vent"   *151*

South Seas Island Resort   *152*
   South Seas Half Jerked Chicken   *153*

Hacienda Petac   *154*
   Bocadita de Res   *155*

Chandler's Bar & Lounge at Cape Rey   *156*
   Beet Chip Crudité with Curried Candied Pecan Dip   *157*

Blantyre   *158*
   Maine Lobster Golden Citrus Salad   *159*

Grand Velas Riviera Nayarit   *160*
   Salad with Blackened Bluefin Tuna and Red Wine Sorbet   *161*

Uniworld Boutique River Cruise Collection   *162*
   Lobster Cocktail "Uniworld"   *163*

W Scottsdale Hotel   *164*
   Fruit Salad   *165*

COCKTAIL ESSENTIALS   167

APPETIZER ESSENTIALS   175

COCKTAIL INDEX   184

APPETIZER INDEX   185

INDEX BY HOTEL/RESORT/CRUISE LINE   186

ABOUT THE AUTHOR   193

Introduction

The skillful art of mixology is trending more than ever throughout the world today. Wherever you travel, there is almost always an inviting lounge where you relax with friends after a day of exploring and shopping.

As with the cuisine and properties featured in our first volume, FIVE STAR RECIPES *from* WORLD FAMOUS HOTELS & RESORTS, you'll find your favorite beverages as well as cocktails unique to their locales and the skills of those tending bar. And, of course, cocktail hours are best enjoyed with an enticing selection of hors d'oeuvres.

The first part of this book brings you signature cocktails served at some of the finest bar lounges in Europe, Africa, Caribbean, USA, Mexico and other points South, South Pacific, plus Asian and European riverways. Recipes for unique and delectable appetizers follow in a separate section. You'll discover that many of the cocktails and appetizers feature exotic ingredients. Some are variations of well-known recipes. Others feature combinations of tastes that may tantalize your adventurous side.

When a particular cocktail or appetizer requires a recipe for an additional ingredient, you will find it in our Cocktail Essentials and Appetizer Essentials sections. And you'll see indexes to help you search by hotel or by recipe.

Stunning photographs, decriptions and stories about these magnificent properties and river cruise lines are also provided for your enjoyment and include websites and phone numbers for your convenience.

À votre santé | Salute | Salud | Prost | L'Chaim | Cheers! To your health!

Linda Lang

Chandler's Bar & Lounge at Cape Rey, Carlsbad, California, USA

Tower Club at lebua
Bangkok, Thailand

On the 51st - 59th floors is the executive, all-suite Tower Club at lebua in the heart of Bangkok's business and shopping areas just a short stroll from the venerable Chao Phraya River. Offering breathtaking views of Bangkok and the Chao Phraya River, each of the 221 enormous suites features a separate bedroom, living room, and kitchenette in a warm, contemporary décor accented by hardwood floors with honey beige and brown furnishings. If you're a fan of the "The Hangover" movie series, you can stay in the lavish three-bedroom Hangover Suite which hosted the cast of The Hangover Part II while they filmed at the hotel.

Room amenities include a non-alcoholic minibar, Nespresso coffee machine, premium bathroom amenities and complimentary access to the intimate, sophisticated Tower Club Lounge which offers continental breakfast, light luncheons, afternoon high tea, canapés and alcoholic and non-alcoholic beverages until 6 pm. Up at Tower Club, you're close to everything including Café Mozu, a state-of-the-art fitness center, outdoor pool and spa, and fully-serviced conference and function rooms. High above on the 67th floor is the regal State Room with its 360-degree view. You are also close to The Dome in lebua's collection of fine dining and bar venues that include the famed Sky Bar, Distil lounge, the celebrated Asian restaurant Breeze, fine Mediterranean dining at the award-winning Sirocco, and Mezzaluna, the award-winning fine-dining mecca known for its innovative cuisine -- all of which are generally considered among the best restaurants and bars in Bangkok.

www.lebua.com/tower-club | Tel: +66 2 624 9555

Tropical Bliss

1.5 oz | 45 ml	Plymouth gin
0.5 oz | 15 ml	lemon juice
0.5 oz | 15 ml	lime cordial
0.5 oz | 15 ml	carbonated water
1 tsp | 33 g	passion fruit powder
2 cubes	jackfruit flavored ice *
1 cube	mango flavored ice **
2 cubes	defused dried apples in rum-flavored ice
4 pcs	dehydrated honey lime wheel

Method:

Fill a mixing glass with flavored jackfruit and mango ice cubes and diffused dried apples.

❖

Add gin, lemon juice and lime cordial and shake well.

❖

Rim a tall glass with dehydrated passion fruit powder and fill with flavored ice.

❖

Pour the mixture into the rimmed glass and top it up with carbonated water.

❖

Garnish with a dehydrated honey lime wheel and a stirrer or swizzle stick.

APPETIZER
Seafood Taco
page 135

* *Jackfruit has a flavor similar to Juicy Fruit gum and can be purchased fresh in Asian and other specialty markets or in jars online.*

** *Put puréed fresh fruit or juice in large ice cube trays and freeze.*

Beau-Rivage Palace
Lausanne, Switzerland

The Beau-Rivage Palace, adjacent to Lake Geneva, is situated on ten acres of private gardens with spectacular views of the Swiss Alps. It recently underwent a US$ 28 million renovation including its 168 guest rooms and suites, La Terrasse restaurant, La Rotonde and the opening of its new signature BAR serving bespoke cocktails. Exuding a retro-chic ambience that is a hallmark of the hotel, period tapestry blends with a transparent onyx bar while antique glass vases top metal and oak shelves embraced by decorative moldings and pillars.

The hotel's award-winning 15,000-square-foot Cinq Mondes Spa contains a fitness room, indoor and outdoor infinity pools, a hot tub and nine treatment rooms. The property's two Michelin starred restaurant Anne-Sophie Pic at the Beau-Rivage Palace features France's only female chef with three Michelin stars. Other amenities include two bars and terraces, two tennis courts and a special program for children.

www.brp.ch | Tel: +41 (0)21 613 33 33

About the BAR...

Head Barman Nicolas Michel, winner of the 2013 Bacardi Legacy Competition in Switzerland, leads a team devoted to the art of the cocktail. With more than 250 quality spirits, every cocktail is an original creation and served in a unique glass. Ice cubes are carved from a large block of ice, and each drink comes with its recipe as a guest souvenir. As a traditional finishing touch, each cocktail is lightly sprayed with a regional fruit-flavored eau de vie from an antique perfume atomizer - a nod to Coco Chanel's frequent visits to the bars of the Beau-Rivage Palace.

City Lights

1 oz | 35 ml	sloe gin
0.35 oz | 10 ml	apricot eau de vie morand (apricot schnapps)
0.35 oz | 10 ml	freshly squeezed lemon juice
1	edible flower for garnish

Method:

Pour the apricot eau de vie morand into a shaker filled with ice.

❖

Add the sloe gin and squeezed lemon. Shake thoroughly for 10 seconds.

❖

Serve in a chilled martini glass. Enhance with a spray of apricot eau de vie and garnish with an edible flower.

Charlie Chaplin & City Lights...

City Lights was created for the opening of the BAR at the Beau-Rivage Palace in 2012. Named after the 1931 silent romantic comedy film written by, directed by, and starring Charlie Chaplin, the cocktail soon became and still remains a popular first choice among guests. As a regular at the Beau-Rivage Palace, Charlie Chaplin would undoubtedly tip his bowler and spin his cane for this delightful blend served martini-style.

QT Sydney
Sydney, Australia

Situated in the restored Gowings and State Theatre buildings in Sydney's central business district, QT Sydney's artful revamp of two historic spaces has brought a unique, hip designer hotel to the city center.

With the gothic façades and features of the buildings carefully returned to their former glory, the hotel's interiors possess cutting-edge art and design featuring LED digital art, bespoke furniture and a strong use of bold colors, making highly distinctive interior design central to the hotel experience.

Located in the heart of the city, QT Sydney is a creative space to dine, drink and live. Opened in September 2012, it is the only hotel in the city to be a member of the exclusive Design Hotels. Dining and relaxation settings include Robert Marchetti's new Gowings Bar & Grill and the Gilt Lounge, Sydney's newest hot bar. The ultra-hip lounge is a popular haunt for both locals and international visitors who enjoy the creative cocktail selection that includes a variety of signature offerings as well as vintage and modern classics.

With a contemporary and, at times, quirky design, all guestrooms feature creature comforts such as 24-hour room service, free WiFi, and most suites also offer an oversized soaking tub. There's also a luxurious day spa.

www.qtsydney.com.au
Tel: +61 2 8262 0000

Barrel-Aged Rendezvous

1.5 oz | 45 ml	high west rendezvous rye
3.5 oz | 10 ml	fernet menta
3.5 oz | 10 ml	demerara sugar*
5 dashes	peach bitters
1	orange twist for garnish

Method:

Stir together first four ingredients and age for eight weeks in French oak.**

❖

Stir mixture over ice in a cocktail shaker and strain into a crystal-cut wine glass.

❖

Garnish with the orange twist.

APPETIZER
Bringing Back the Vol-au-Vent
page 151

* A large-grained, semi-crunchy raw sugar that originated in Guyana and is now produced in Hawaii, Mexico, India, and other countries. Also known as tubinado sugar in many markets. Can be ordered online.

** If you don't have a French Oak barrel, you can use French Oak WineStix which can be ordered online at www.winestix.com, http://morewinemaking.com/search?search=French+Oak+WineStix, and other sites.

SIGNATURE COCKTAILS & APPETIZERS *from* AROUND THE WORLD

THE MILESTONE HOTEL
LONDON, ENGLAND

The Milestone Hotel, an exquisite award-winning five-star Grade II Listed Hotel overlooking Kensington Palace and Gardens, is just minutes from the Royal Albert Hall and the West End.

Each of its beautifully-appointed 44 guest rooms, 12 luxury suites and six apartments is a work of art graced with fine fabrics, antique furnishings, rare artwork and fresh flowers. No two are alike. The latest 21st-century technology, placed throughout the property, includes complimentary high-speed wireless Internet and interactive TV with movies on demand. Upon arrival, butlers provide a complimentary glass of champagne (or any other drink of choice) and offer to unpack all bags.

Facilities include Stables Bar, Cheneston's Restaurant, a fire-lit lounge, heated resistance pool, gym, sauna, and chauffeur-driven Bentley to whisk you to the city sights. Children and pets also receive the royal treatment.

www.milestonehotel.com |
Tel: +44 (0)20 7917 1000

About The Milestone Old Fashioned...

After looking at the many bars in London, the Milestone decided to create its own unique series of three old fashioned cocktails using whisky, rum and tequila which have been barrel rested in-house for two weeks with a mix of maple syrup and neutral spirit. They also produce their own homemade bitters, adding authenticity to their old fashioned cocktails. This method of creating this fine cocktail is true to its origin in 1806. Revisited classic recipes reminiscent of the 20's, 40's, 50's and 60's create a cocktail menu with a delightful retro feel.

The 'smoking' concept was started years ago by a Milestone bartender. With a smoking gun (hand-held smoker) he purloined from the kitchen along with some wood chips and a glass dome, he produced the smoking effect which you still experience today.

The Milestone Old Fashioned

2 oz | 60 ml	aged spirit (rested whisky, rum or tequila)
1	sugar cube
2-3 dashes	rose bitters
1	large Ice cube
1	orange peel
1	orange slice and a marasca cherry (large Italian cherries soaked in maraschino) to garnish.
4 oz | 133 gr	wood chips

Tools:
Smoking gun (handheld food smoker) glass jar or bottle with tight fitting lid

Method:
Place sugar in a mixing glass and soak with 2-3 dashes of the rose bitters.

Add an orange peel and 0.5 oz |10 ml of the chosen spirit.

Work the mixture with a cocktail muddler* or mixing tool to dissolve the sugar.

When the sugar is dissolved, add the rest of the spirit (1.5 oz | 50 ml), plenty of ice and stir well.

Pour mixture into the glass container, add smoke from the smoking gun for a few seconds, quickly seal container and wait until the ice begins to melt.

When you have enough ice melting and chilling the drink, pour the mixture over a big mound of crushed ice in an old fashioned glass.

Garnish with a slice of orange and a marasca cherry.

A bartender's pestle used to smash ingredients for cocktails such as the mojito and old fashioned.

SIGNATURE COCKTAILS & APPETIZERS *from* AROUND THE WORLD

Hotel Hassler Roma
Rome, Italy

Set atop the Spanish Steps with a panoramic view of the city, Hotel Hassler Roma has been a favorite haven for celebrities, royalty and discerning travelers for more than a century. It was home for Audrey Hepburn during the filming of "Roman Holiday"; Prince Rainier and Grace Kelly honeymooned here; and Princess Diana once told Hassler owner and general manager Roberto Wirth that she had enjoyed the world's best "Bellini" here and complimented him upon the Hassler Bar's signature Veruschka cocktail, the renowned invigorating mix of pomegranate juice and champagne, featured on the next page.

Each of the Hassler's 96 rooms, 14 of which are suites, is individually designed with a stunning blend of classic elegance with contemporary amenities. Highlights include dining in the Michelin-starred 6th floor restaurant, Imàgo, with its panoramic views over the city and soft music enhancing the romantic Italian dining experience. Salone Eva is another favorite place for a quiet rendezvous while the Palm Court offers informal dining as does the neighboring Hassler-owned Il Palazzetto, a hotel, wine bar and place for special events.

In addition, you'll discover the Hassler's Amorvero SPA noted for its relaxing ambience as well as extensive selection of beauty treatments, massages, and private appointments for the sauna, steam bath, and solarium. The fitness center is a complete training facility with cardio fitness machines, weight room and the possibility of a personal trainer.

www.hotelhasslerroma.com | Tel: +39 06 699340

Veruschka Cocktail

30%	freshley-squeezed pomegranate juice
70%	champagne

Method:

Squeeze the pomegranate with a hand juicer.

❖

Filter and place the juice in the fridge for about three hours to chill thoroughly.

❖

Pour into a champagne flute and top off with champagne.

Hassler Owner and General Manager Roberto Wirth (L) with Head Barman Luigi Berardi.

About the Hassler Bar...

Behind Salone Eva is the legendary Hassler Bar. A perfect place for an aperitif or an after-dinner-drink, you are immersed in a luxurious, relaxing ambience complete with delightful piano music. Here you enjoy the atmosphere of an English Club, while being well looked after by head barman Luigi Berardi.

Hotel Casa 425
Ontario, California, USA

Hotel Casa 425, a stylish boutique hotel in the heart of Claremont Village, is on the town square within steps of fine restaurants, cafes, nightlife, boutiques and art galleries. Also nearby are the prestigious Claremont Colleges, and the Ontario International Airport is but a short drive.

Featuring modern Mexican design, the hotel's 28 spacious guestrooms overlook an interior, open-air courtyard lined with trees, tiny lights and fountains. Rooms offer king or two queen beds, oversized soaking tubs, fine linens, spa-quality bath amenities, flat panel TVs, refrigerators with free bottled water, complimentary coffee and tea and free wireless Internet access. Décor is modern and bright with vibrant colors and original art. You can also enjoy a continental breakfast daily as well as the hotel's bicycles to peddle around Claremont.

In the Hotel Casa 425 Lounge, there's a menu of savory small plates as well as innovative cocktails. Seating is either indoors -- where a full bar and cozy fireplace awaits -- or outside around the glass fire pits. Happy Hour is Monday through Saturday, 4 pm to 7 pm, with specially-priced drinks and appetizers. On Sunday, Happy Hour is extended to 9 pm. Throughout the year, the Lounge hosts special events from the popular Vino + Vinyasa wine and yoga afternoons to live music in the courtyard.

www.casa425.com | Tel: +1 866 450 0425

Very Berry Spicy Margarita

Courtesy of Jason Cerswell, Lounge Manager, Hotel Casa 425 + Lounge

2 oz | 60 ml	tequila
1 oz | 30 ml	fresh lime juice
1 oz | 30 ml	agave nectar
1	blackberry
2	raspberries
1/4 in | 6 mm	wheel of fresh jalapeño*
	margarita salt

Method:

Muddle (mash) berries and jalapeño in a cocktail shaker.

❖

Add agave nectar, lime juice and tequila.

❖

Add ice and shake hard for 5-6 seconds.

❖

Salt the outside rim of a chilled rocks glass with margarita salt** and fill with fresh ice.

❖

Strain the mixture into the glass.

❖

Garnish with a lime wedge, jalapeno disc and a blackberry.

* Slice 1/4 inch thick wheels horizontally, not lengthwise.
** Rub the outside of the rim with a piece of lime. Dip the top edge of the glass into container of margarita salt and twist slightly to coat. Wipe away any salt that sticks to the inside of the glass. Can be done in advance and kept in freezer.

APPETIZER
Esquitres (Roasted Corn Dip)
page 127

SIGNATURE COCKTAILS & APPETIZERS *from* AROUND THE WORLD

Regent Berlin
Berlin, Germany

A haven of elegance in a bustling metropolis, the Regent Berlin is located on the beautiful Gendarmenmarkt square in the historical center of the capital with splendid views of two 18th-century cathedrals and the old Concert Hall. The most important museums, numerous luxury boutiques, and the famed Friedrichstrasse shopping mile are just a stroll away as are several of the most significant sights including the Brandenburg Gate, Reichstag and Opera.

According to the Travellers´ Choice Awards published in January 2015 by *Trip Advisor*, Regent Berlin is named the "Best Hotel in Berlin" and one of the "Top 10 Hotels in Germany." It offers 156 luxurious guest rooms, which are among the largest in the city, 39 suites, and a magnificent presidential suite on the top floor. Many of the rooms, which combine classic elegance with high technology, also have balconies. To relax between shopping, business and sightseeing activities, the Regent Health Club offers state-of-the-art exercise equipment, separate women's and men's saunas, a spa, and body massages by skilled therapists.

At the Michelin-starred restaurant Fischers Fritz, chef de cuisine Christian Lohse features gourmet fish and other seafood specialties. The critically-acclaimed chef was awarded a Michelin star just six months after opening the restaurant. Lohse's dedication to his craft placed him at the forefront of Berlin's culinary world when he became the first chef in Berlin in 13 years to merit 2 Michelin stars. He's maintained his crown as Berlin's 2 Michelin-starred chef for his classic French cuisine with a contemporary twist for the past eight consecutive years.

www.regenthotels.com/berlin |
Tel: +0049 (0)30 20 33 8

Espressotini

1 oz | 30 ml		Russian standard vodka
1 oz | 30 ml		homemade coffee liqueur*
1 dash		sugar syrup
1		double espresso (hot)
3		coffee beans
		ice cubes to fill a shaker

Method:

Pour the Russian standard vodka, homemade coffee liqueur, hot double espresso and dash of sugar syrup in a shaker filled with ice cubes.

❖

Shake vigorously for at least 10 to 15 seconds to get a strong, solid foam.

❖

Strain mixture into a chilled martini glass, removing the ice. After about 10 seconds, the foam is set.

❖

Top foam with three coffee beans for decoration.

* See Cocktail Essentials.

About the Bar Team...

The bar team has been working together since 2013 creating their own fusion cocktails and new interpretations of classic drinks. From left: Benjamin Sperling, Bar Supervisor since 2009; Timo Haeberle, Bartender since 2010; Kevin Tappe, Commis de Bar since 2012.

Montague on the Gardens
London, England

The Montague on the Gardens in elegant Bloomsbury provides us with a distant echo of the antics of the rascally Ralph, Duke of Montagu, who came by this land in a very devious manner. The story begins with a 'crack-brained, addle-pated fellow' named Christopher Monck, 2nd Earl of Albemarle, whose father had been the chief player in restoring Charles II to the throne of England in 1660. The houses of Montague Street were constructed between 1803 and 1806 over the gardens of Montagu House and today almost every one on the terrace is listed Grade II by English Heritage as a building of 'architectural and/or historic interest'.

Red Carnation Hotels took over the Montague Hotel in 1996 and transformed it into a four star deluxe Georgian townhouse hideaway in the heart of the city that combines up-to-the-minute sophistication with ample old-world charm. Over recent years, the hotel has undergone various refurbishment programmes. In 2007, it added The Guv'nor's Suite, a two-bedroom apartment which epitomises design chic with its marble corridor, faux suede walls and under-floor heating.

www.montaguehotel.com | Tel: +44 (0) 20 7612 8416

About The Terrace Bar...

No great hotel is complete without an intimate, first-class bar where you can while away the time in quiet contemplation or in good company. The Terrace Bar at The Montague on the Gardens is just such an oasis, tucked snugly away from the city streets. Here you'll find comfortable, quiet and cozy corners, a variety of bar snacks and meals complementing the tantalizing talents of The Terrace Bar's cocktail mixologist. Live entertainment is provided every Monday to Saturday evening from 7 pm until 10 pm. The Terrace Bar opens up onto the Cigar Terrace overlooking the private gardens of the Bedford Estate where you can enjoy a fabulous al fresco breakfast or lunch.

Thyme Sloes Down

(sloe gin and thyme sour)

1.75 oz | 50 ml	sip smith sloe gin
1 oz | 30 ml	fresh lime juice
0.5 to 0.75 oz | 10-20 ml	sugar syrup
1	large egg white
3 sprigs	fresh thyme + 1 for garnish
1	twist of lime for garnish

Method:

Chill an old fashioned glass.

Muddle* the fresh thyme in a shaker glass to release the oils.

Add the sloe gin, lime juice and sugar syrup.

Shake vigorously for 10-15 seconds.

Strain into one side of the shaker to remove the ice. Discard ice.

Add 1 egg white and dry shake for froth.

Strain into the chilled old fashioned glass with 3-4 ice cubes.

Garnish with lime twist around a sprig of thyme.

* Use a bartender's muddler or pestle to smash ingredients.

SIGNATURE COCKTAILS & APPETIZERS *from* AROUND THE WORLD

BBAR
London, England

Bbar is a South African-styled watering hole just two minutes from Victoria Station. With its vintage photographs of big game, faux giraffe skin fabrics, ethnic carvings, leopard-spotted lampshades and polished zebrano wood table tops, it's a funky mix of safari chic and colonial cool.

The menu is international with a strong South African accent lent by dishes like springbok fillet, grilled boerewors sausages and bobotie spring rolls. The two bars serve an impressive 110 wines (over 50 by the glass) from an eclectic list of old and new world producers. Passionate mixologists prepare over 60 cocktails, from the classics to the more exotic, while the warm, relaxed service creates an invitingly intimate atmosphere.

bbar is also a great venue for celebrating all manner of private parties. With the two bars and a variety of levels, it offers versatile options including exclusive 'drinks & canapés' functions for 250 people and private dining for 100 guests with bespoke menus.

43 Below is an intimate lower bar that can be booked separately. With its own sound system, comfortable leather sofas and soft lighting, it's perfect for private groups of up to 70 guests.

www.bbarlondon.com | Tel: +020 7958 7000

Bushman's Delight

1 oz | 30 ml	courvoisier brandy
0.7 oz | 20 ml	krupnik honey liquor
3.3 oz | 100 ml	savanna dry cider
4	thyme stems plus one for garnish
1	honeycomb cube* plus piece for garnish

Method:

Muddle thyme, add honeycomb, brandy and krupnik.

❖

Shake, strain over cubed ice in a sling or pilsner glass.

❖

Top up with savanna cider.

❖

Garnish with thyme stalk and honeycomb on top.

* Raw honeycomb can be purchased in specialty stores or online.

The Lafayette Hotel
San Diego, California, USA

The Lafayette Hotel is a charming California boutique hotel that was once a haven for celebrities like Bob Hope and Ava Gardner. Built in a grand colonial style by developer Larry Imig, this 1946 historic landmark was the San Diego Chargers' first headquarters when it was owned by Conrad Hilton. The hotel's legendary Mississippi Ballroom was also the location for the famed "You've Lost That Lovin' Feelin'" scene in the movie *Top Gun*.

Located in the vibrant North Park San Diego community, the hotel is renowned for its laid-back medley of history, playfulness, and casual ambience. It offers 131 rooms in four categories, a junior Olympic-sized swimming pool, fitness room, two restaurants, an improv comedy theatre, business center and 15,000 square feet of flexible meeting space.

The restaurant and bar were newly rebranded as HOPE 46 Classic American Cuisine -- "HOPE" referring to Frank Hope, the building's architect; Bob Hope, the hotel's first guest; and the hope all Americans shared when their families returned from the war. Adorned with a large collection of black and white photos, vintage memorabilia, and retro Americana, HOPE 46 tells the tale of American history through its cuisine. The restaurant reinvents classic dishes inspired by American immigrants, and the bar presents handcrafted, pre-prohibition era cocktails made with the finest ingredients and spirits.

www.lafayettehotelsd.com | Tel: +1 610 296 2101

The Smoking Red Rose

by Greg LaChance, Craft Cocktail Creator

0.5 oz | 15 ml	green chartreuse
2 oz | 60 ml	redbreast Irish whiskey
0.25 oz | 7.5 ml	simple syrup
1	jumbo ice ball
2 sprigs	rosemary

Method:

Light one sprig of rosemary with a hand-torch and place in a goblet glass.

❖

Cover the glass with a dish to retain smoke. This will flavor the inside of the glass.

❖

Fill a mixing glass with ice, and pour in the chartreuse, redbreast and simple syrup.

❖

Stir and strain over a large spherical ice ball in the goblet.

❖

Garnish with a sprig of fresh rosemary.

Greg LaChance, Craft Cocktail Creator

APPETIZER
Pacific Bay Scallop Burschetta
page 129

SIGNATURE COCKTAILS & APPETIZERS *from* AROUND THE WORLD

BROWN TLV URBAN HOTEL
Tel Aviv, Israel

In the heart of Tel Aviv's urban scene at the crossroads of the charming Neve Tzedek quarter and trendy Rothschild Boulevard, the Brown TLV Urban Hotel is an ideal choice for the seasoned business traveler as well as the lifestyle-driven individual eager to access this vibrant city. Arts, culture, dining and nightlife are just outside the door and the beach is but a 10-minute walk. The hotel caters to the value-minded, yet stylishly discerning guest. Combining unique retro design, trendy ambiance and personalized service, Brown TLV is an award-winning hotel recommended by international magazines such as *NY Times, Wallpaper, Condé Nast Traveler, Vogue* and *Time Magazine*.

The boutique property offers 30 stylish, well-appointed rooms carefully designed to maximize your comfort. There's a beautiful sundeck overlooking the city, a spa, business facilities, and two classy bars as well as complimentary bicycles and free access to a nearby high-end gym.

Brown's guests enjoy a diverse local experience with breakfast being served in several neighboring cafes, each a popular Tel Aviv establishment. Brown TLV is the city's only member of the world's top boutique hotel brand Design Hotels.

www.browntlv.com | Tel: + 03 717 0200

Orient Express

1.35 oz | 40 ml	Bombay sapphire gin
0.7 oz | 20 ml	cointreau
1 oz | 30 ml	fresh lemon juice
1.35 oz | 40 ml	homemade earl grey infusion*
	flamed rosemary, lemon peel and cherry for garnish

Method:
Pour the first four ingredients into a shaker and shake well.

Pour over ice in a rocks glass and add the garnishes.

Combine 8.5 oz | 250 ml gin and 2 tbsp | 5 g of loose leaf earl grey tea in a covered glass container. Let steep for 304 hours, no longer. Strain into a clean bottle.

THE GREENWICH HOTEL
NEW YORK CITY, NEW YORK, USA

Located in Tribeca, one of New York's most desirable neighborhoods, The Greenwich Hotel was created for comfort and hand-crafted beauty by its owners, Robert De Niro and Ira Drukier along with Richard Born and Raphael De Niro. Talented artisans from around the world fashioned a warm, richly-layered environment that celebrates craftsmanship and natural materials. You'll find hand-loomed Tibetan silk rugs, hand-laid Moroccan tile, Italian Carrara marble, English leather settees, and beds from Duxiana in Sweden.

The hotel offers 88 rooms including 13 suites — some with saunas or soaking tubs, others with working fireplaces — of which no two are alike. Accommodations also feature HD flat screen TVs, iPod docking stations, and complimentary wireless Internet. DVD players, laptop computers, faxes, and pre-loaded iPods are also available upon request as are pet-friendly rooms at no additional charge.

Amenities also include a private drawing room which leads to a courtyard where guests can dine from Locanda Verde's menu beneath latticed vines. Adjoining the hotel Locanda Verde, a casual neighborhood Italian inn serving chef Andrew Carmellini's creative Italian fare. The Shibui Spa houses five treatment rooms, a fitness center, and lantern-lit lounge under the roof of a reconstructed wood and bamboo farmhouse --a true haven for relaxation.

thegreenwichhotel.com | Tel: +1 212 941 8900

Agri Cola

0.5 oz | 15 ml	rhum clément prèmier cannes
0.5 oz | 15 ml	barboncourt rhum
0.5 oz | 15 ml	avuá cachaça*
0.5 oz | 15 ml	lime juice
0.5 oz | 15 ml	house-made spiced grenadine**
splash	chinotto
slice	lime

Method:
Mix the first five ingredients and pour over ice in a highball glass. Add a splash of chinotto.

❖

Garnish with a slice of lime or lemon.

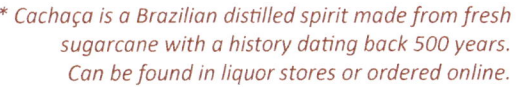

APPETIZER
Crab Crostino
page 125

* Cachaça is a Brazilian distilled spirit made from fresh sugarcane with a history dating back 500 years. Can be found in liquor stores or ordered online.

** For recipe, see Cocktail Essentials.

SIGNATURE COCKTAILS & APPETIZERS *from* AROUND THE WORLD

Royal Blues Hotel
Deerfield Beach, Florida, USA

A luxury art boutique property located in Deerfield Beach, Florida, the Royal Blues Hotel is an oceanfront escape where you discover an authentic adventure along Florida's Gold Coast's rich American culture and history. Boasting lots of local attractions, you can relax after a day of exploring on beautiful white sand beaches adjacent to the fishing pier.

Its contemporary design applies fluid architecture framed by clean, flowing lines to luxury accommodations outfitted in subtle combinations of leather, wood, and marble to craft spaces reminiscent of a modern luxury yacht. Each guest room is completely unique in personality and style. In addition to the terrace rooms, one-bedroom suite, and two bedrooms adjoined by a shared living space, there is a spacious penthouse suite complete with a bar and exceptional balcony view. The hotel also features original works of art in every guest room to complement the stunning ocean views of bordering beaches.

Upon arrival, you'll find lush robes, towels, and slippers as well as beach and pool towels. Other amenities include signature scent candles, gourmet snack and minibar, state-of-the-art technology including LED HDTVs with attached sound bars, and secure high-speed WiFi.

Royal Blues is also home to a casually elegant wine lounge in the interior lobby as well as Chanson Restaurant, a fine dining experience that showcases the freshest seafood available in innovative menus in the style of "Cuisine Du Monde."

royalblueshotel.com | Tel: +1 954 857 2929

Fluffy Bunny Cocktail

1 oz	30 ml	Ocean's vodka
2 oz	60 ml	cold brewed Rabbit Coffee
1 oz	30 ml	Bailey's Irish cream
0.5 oz	15 ml	kalua
		chocolate sauce for garnish
		raspberry for garnish
		chocolate powder

Method:

In a cocktail mixing glass filled with ice, combine the vodka, coffee, Bailey's and kalua

❖

Shake hard to create a nice froth.

❖

In a cold martini glass, pour a swirl of chocolate sauce around the glass.

❖

Add the well-shaken cocktail.

❖

Place a raspberry on top of the froth.

❖

Finish the presentation with a light dusting of chocolate powder.

APPETIZER

Diver Scallops with Carnaroli Risotto

page 145

About the Fluffy Bunny Cocktail...

The Fluffy Bunny was created after meeting between Royal Blues General Manager Claude Dubois and the owner of Rabbit Coffee & Co, a local coffee roasting company located in Palm Beach. In keeping with the hotel's commitment to support local businesses, Claude Dubois decided to have Rabbit Coffee featured at the hotel. It was during Easter that the bar team attempted to create some after-dinner cocktails with coffee, and after multiple attempts, the Fluffy Bunny Cocktail was born on April 3rd, just two days prior to Easter.

SIGNATURE COCKTAILS & APPETIZERS *from* AROUND THE WORLD

The Rubens
London, England

The Rubens at the Palace, opposite the Royal Mews of Buckingham Palace, is moments from London's top shops, restaurants and Victoria Station. First opening as a hotel in 1912, the property primarily hosted the debutantes and high-society guests of Buckingham Palace. Today, The Rubens is still rated as one of the highest four-star London hotels, and the magnificent building has retained its original historical splendor.

Each of the 143 deluxe guest rooms, eight royal rooms, 10 luxurious suites and two self-contained apartments are beautifully furnished. Many have views overlooking the Royal Mews, and traditional elegance blends seamlessly with the latest modern amenities including complimentary high-speed Internet access, entertainment system with interactive TV, a huge selection of on-demand movies, and a music library.

There is fine dining in two elegantly-furnished restaurants — the Old Master's which offers succulent roasts and international fare while the Library Restaurant serves award-winning English cuisine. The Palace Lounge and Cavalry Bar are extremely popular among guests and locals alike. A favorite spot for afternoon tea is the Palace Lounge, a bright open room with sweeping views of The Royal Mews and the Queen's stables.

There is also a dedicated children's concierge as well as a pet concierge to assist families visiting London.

www.rubenshotel.com | Tel: +44 (0)20 7834 6600

Rubens Royal Blush

1 oz	30 ml	amaretto
2 tsp	10 ml	strawberry puree
1 oz	30 ml	vodka
	dash	grenadine
	dash	cream
	1/2	lime
	1/2	strawberry for garnish

Method:

Shake all ingredients with ice in a cocktail shaker.

❖

Shake until a good froth has developed.

❖

Strain into a daiquiri glass.

❖

Garnish with half a strawberry.

About the Bar...

The Cavalry Bar provides a welcoming atmosphere with interesting military artefacts displayed around the area that recall key historical events throughout the rule of the British Empire. In the evenings, a pianist provides soothing background music starting at 6:30 pm. The extensive bar menu features a wide selection of beers, wines and spirits including Guy Cadel Champagne served by the glass or a warming 10-year-old Inverarity single malt whisky bottled in Speyside, Scotland especially for The Rubens.

Bar manager Steve Jones oversees your pleasure whether it be enjoying a signature cocktail, sampling some delectable bar food, or just relaxing with a nice cup of tea.

W Scottsdale Hotel
Scottsdale, Arizona, USA

Scottsdale's social scene has exploded in the past decade. Today, the city is often considered the desert version of Miami's South Beach. The first W Hotel in Arizona, W Scottsdale anchors the new nightlife scene in the heart of the city. This unique AAA Four Diamond trendy oasis is also within walking distance of a wide variety of excellent restaurants, designer shops at Scottsdale Fashion Square Mall, the eclectic arts district, galleries, waterfront overlooking the Arizona Canal across from the mall, and much more.

W Scottsdale's innovative design blends and urban sophistication in its public rooms and 230 guest rooms including 33 lavish suites. You can dine at the hotel's popular Sushi Roku restaurant, relax in the fashionable W Living Room Lounge with its wide choice of signature cocktails, and mingle at the sophisticated indoor/outdoor bar or Shade Lounge while a DJ spins the hottest beats. You can also spend the day poolside at WET on the second floor, energize at FIT Fitness®, and find renewal at Bliss® Scottsdale Spa. To golf, explore Camelback Mountain and other sites, consult the concierge.

Additional signature services and amenities include the Whatever/Whenever® concierge service, Wheels℠, WIRED Business Center, and P.A.W. – Pets Are Welcome™.

www.wscottsdalehotel.com |
Tel: +1 877 W HOTELS (9 468357)

Vitamin W Cocktail

1.5 oz | 45 ml	Ketel One oranje*
0.5 oz | 15 ml	chambord
2.5 oz | 75 ml	cranberry juice
1.5 oz | 45 ml	fresh orange juice
5-6	fresh raspberries
2	orange wedges
2	lime wedges

Method:

Muddle the raspberries, 1 orange wedge, and 1 lime wedge with the chambord in a pint glass.

Fill the glass with ice. Add the Ketel One oranje, cranberry juice, and orange juice.

Cover and shake well to fully mix the ingredients.

Pour mixture into the desired glass and garnish with a fresh raspberry, orange and lime wedges.

APPETIZER
Fruit Salad
page 165

* Ketel One vodka infused for at least 24 hours (steeped or soaked without boiling) with valencia and mandarin oranges.

The Bungalow
Santa Monica, California, USA

The Bungalow, one of the trendiest spots in Southern California, was created by the rich imagination of Brent Bolthouse. Known for its stunning, upscale rustic décor, the atmosphere features expansive ocean views, lush gardens, sweeping decks and outdoor seating around cozy fire pits — all of which radiate the charm of another era.

This is not just another bar. The Bungalow is where you meet with friends after work to relax in an inviting, beach-house setting and catch up over a frosted margarita or sangria as the sun turns the sky blazing orange before sinking into the ocean. The Bungalow Is where 20 somethings take over from the early crowd about 9 pm and make it their place. The music embraces everything from old Motown, '60s soul, Donovan, and the Black Keys to the Edward Sharpes of the 21st century. You won't find a dance floor or have to outshout ear-shattering music; yet The Bungalow is one of Southern California's hottest multigenerational nightlife venues.

Specialties of the inside and outside bars include tequila and mezcal cocktails, The Bungalow's signature margaritas and Bitchin' Sangria featured on the next page. In lieu of formal dining, The Bungalow has a close relationship with the adjacent Miramar Hotel's FIG Restaurant chef Yousef Ghalaini who provides an exclusive bar menu that includes burgers, tacos and its popular guacamole and chips.

www.thebungalowSM.com | Tel: +1 310 899 8530

Bitchin' Sangria

1 bottle	California pinot noir	1/4	pineapple, roughly chopped
1/2 bottle	California cabernet sauvignon	1	apple, roughly chopped*
8 oz | 237 ml	Oro pisco	1	orange roughly chopped
8 oz | 237 ml	St. Germain liqueur	1	grapefruit roughly chopped
6 oz | 177 ml	agave nectar	1	mango roughly chopped
4 dashes	Regan's orange bitters #6	2	nectarines or plums, when in season

Method:
Combine all ingredients together in a large pitcher, cover and store in a refrigerator overnight.

❖

To serve, fill a wine glass with ice and add 5 oz | 148 ml of the sangria and garnish with seasonal fruit.

*Pink Lady or Cripp's Pink, if available.

Chandler's Bar & Lounge at Cape Rey
Carlsbad, California, USA

In keeping with its casual California coastal setting, Chandler's Bar and Lounge is a popular gathering spot offering a daily happy hour with live music on weekends. With its lively bar scene transcending to table service and closing with the late night-capping crowd, this bar centric restaurant is a great spot to relax and catch up with good friends and entertain out of town guests.

The beverage program features three distinct elements. With San Diego being a leader in the craft beer movement, there's a nice selection of local craft beers. The menu also features specialty signature cocktails creatively inspired by old fashioned classics as well as new innovative mixology. Among the offerings are crafted creations representing the spirits indigenous to this region such as the Chandler's margarita, cranberry caipirinha, and beet infused rosemary ginger cocktail featured on the next page. Always present is an emphasis on fresh seasonal ingredients and garnishes.

The wine program focuses upon smaller vineyards with limited production from Central California offering a large variety of choices of excellent quality less known to the general public as well as a selection of more well-known labels.

www.chandlerscarlsbad.com | Tel: +1 760 683 5500

Beet Infused Rosemary Ginger Cocktail

1.5 oz | 45 ml	rosemary-peppercorn-beet infused vodka*
0.5 oz | 15 ml	canton ginger liqueur
0.25 oz | 7.5 ml	lime juice
0.25 oz | 7.5 ml	simple syrup
dash	club soda

Method:

Add first 4 ingredients to cocktail shaker and fill with ice.

❖

Shake vigorously and strain into a collins glass filled with ice.

❖

Top with club soda.

❖

Garnish with beet chip crudité from appetizer* *(Optional)*

APPETIZER
Beet Chip Crudité with Curried Pecan Dip
page 157

* For recipe, see Cocktail Essentials.

SIGNATURE COCKTAILS & APPETIZERS *from* AROUND THE WORLD

Tuscany, Italy

Palazzo Avino
Ravello, Italy

High on the Amalfi Coast south of Naples with panoramic views of the Mediterranean Sea and charming little town of Ravello, Palazzo Avino is a shining jewel surrounded by profusions of flowers and pastel-painted houses offering a serene, luxurious haven from a busy world.

Originally a 12th Century villa built for an esteemed Italian noble family, the property and its 32 rooms have been tastefully refurbished to the highest standards while retaining its medieval and baroque features. Palazzo Avino has been recognized internationally with many prestigious awards including being been named one of the best hotels in the world by both *Travel + Leisure* and *Condé Nast Traveler* magazines.

The hotel's brand new Lobster and Martini Bar boasts a list of around 100 different martinis including the Palazzo Avino Mule, a creative version of the famous Moscow mule. It's a wonderful prelude to dining in the Michelin-starred restaurant, Rossellinis -- a gastronomic experience not to be missed.

Palazzo Avino also has a new private beach club appropriately called Clubhouse By the Sea which offers complete ocean access, a casual restaurant, and small swimming pool. Reserved exclusively for hotel guests, it sits at the base of the mountain with complimentary day-long shuttle service to and from the hotel.

www.palazzoavino.com | Tel: +39 089 818181

Sunlight Martini

Recipe by Barman Stefano Amato

3 parts	vodka fragranced with Amalfitan lemons peels*
2 parts	homemade fennel seed and ginger root alcoholate**
3 drops	dry vermouth
	lemon twist

Method:
Pour the first three ingredients gently over ice in a mixing glass and stir carefully for a few seconds.

❖

Strain and pour into a 5 oz | 148 ml martini glass and garnish with a twist of lemon.

APPETIZER
King Lobster on bread "Pizzaiola" Style
page 141

*An infusion of the peels of three lemons immersed in 34 oz | 1 liter of belvedere vodka for 24 hours.
**See Cocktail Essentials.

SIGNATURE COCKTAILS & APPETIZERS *from* AROUND THE WORLD

THE GREENBRIER
SULPHUR SPRINGS, WEST VIRGINIA, USA

One of the oldest resorts in America, The Greenbrier has been welcoming guests since 1778. Known as "America's Resort," it encompasses more than 10,000 private acres in the foothills of West Virginia's Allegheny Mountains and features four golf courses, a new championship tennis stadium, a 40,000-square-foot spa, 13 restaurants and bars, and more.

Named the "Resort of the Century" by *Andrew Harper's Hideaway Report* in 1999, The Greenbrier continues to earn top ratings year after year from T*ravel + Leisure, Condé Nast Traveler, Huffington Post, USA TODAY* and many more. Combining the graciousness of the past with the conveniences and comforts of today, this internationally-renowned property offers 710 rooms including 33 suites and 96 guest and estate homes, 10 lobbies, 40+ meeting rooms and conference center.

www.greenbrier.com | Tel: +1 855 453 4858

History of The Greenbrier's Mint Julep...

The Mint Julep at The Greenbrier goes back almost to the resort's beginnings. The oldest account book dates from 1816 and reveals that guests ordered "julips" at a cost of 25 cents per drink. When the popular writer Charles Dudley Warner described The Greenbrier in 1886, he noted that travelers were met by attendants "who avowed that there was no time of day or night when a mint julep or any other necessity of life would not be forthcoming at a moment's warning." By 1914, the mint julep was such a staple that a recipe for the drink appeared on The Greenbrier's souvenir calendar.

The Greenbrier's Original Mint Julep

12-15	fresh mint leaves
1 oz | 30 ml	simple syrup
2 oz | 60 ml	Maker's Mark bourbon
	sprig of mint dusted with powdered sugar

Method:

Muddle mint leaves with simple syrup in a mint julep cup.*

❖

Fill cup with crushed ice.

❖

Add the bourbon.

❖

Stir once or twice.

❖

Garnish with the sprig of mint dusted with powdered sugar.

* Mint Julep cups are available in stores and online.

Blantyre
Lenox, Massachusetts, USA

A secluded, romantic, renowned Relais et Chateaux country house in the heart of the Berkshires, Blantyre embodies the eloquent lifestyle of a bygone era. This Forbes Five Star Tudor manor, which also has numerous accolades from Condé Nast, Travel + Leisure among others, has 19 exquisitely-furnished rooms and suites in the Main House and Carriage House plus four cottages complete every amenity.

Just a short walk from the Main House in the meadows is the Potting Shed Spa offering a large menu of treatments as well a recreational area with a common sauna, oversized hot tub, steam room, fitness area and seasonal outside pool. A wealth of outdoor activities includes, tennis, golf and winter sports such as cross country skiing and ice skating.

Dining is a very special event at Blantyre. Late every afternoon, the Main House undergoes a transformation as the staff prepares for the delightful dining experience complete with beautiful linens, sterling silver, fine china, crystal, fresh flowers, and beautiful music filling the air as the candles are lit. One of the best kept secrets is the wine cellar. With over 10,000 bottles, the wine list is one of the finest in the Berkshires. The sommeliers and wine director can arrange a private cellar tour and wine tasting.

www.blantyre.com | Tel: +1 844 881 0104

Gilded Age Cocktail

champagne
Pimm's liqueur
1   brown sugar cube, approx. 0.5 in | 1.3 cm square
1   orange twist

Method:

In a champagne flute, place 1 brown sugar cube in bottom of glass.

❖

Cover 1/2 of the sugar cube with Pimm's.

❖

Pour champagne over the mixture and garnish with an orange twist.

APPETIZER
Maine Lobster Golden Citrus Salad
page 159

SIGNATURE COCKTAILS & APPETIZERS *from* AROUND THE WORLD

Wharekauhau Lodge
Pallister Bay, New Zealand

Winner of Andrew Harper's Grand Award in 1998 and 2004 and *Wine Spectator's* Best of Award of Excellence in 2003 and 2004, Wharekauhau Lodge is an exclusive resort at Palliser Bay which redefines the word "unique." Recently ranked one of the top ten international hideaway resorts, Wharekauhau offers you the chance immerse yourself in New Zealand country hospitality and scenic grandeur.

This remarkable resort is on a 5500 acre working sheep station on New Zealand's dramatic eastern coast near Wellington. Wharekauhau heralds a new era of elegance and graciousness without losing the warmth, conviviality and intimacy of country hospitality. It is here that you can experience the true spirit of New Zealand in remarkable style.

The lodge is modelled along the lines of an Edwardian country mansion with a grand hall, open wood burning fireplaces, mullioned windows, and country-style kitchen. The 13 private guest suites offer solitude and comfort in splendid yet unpretentious surroundings and are placed throughout the grounds to take advantage of the stunning coastal views of the bay.

Year round, you can experience the solitude of this spectacularly rugged landscape, pursue a fascinating range of outdoor activities, and enjoy the luxury of Wharekauhau's spectacular setting, savour local wines and superb cuisine made from the finest and freshest ingredients.

www.wharekauhau.co.nz | Tel: +64 6 3077581

The Perfect Wharekauhau Gin Martini

2 oz | 60 ml	lighthouse gin
splash	martini dry vermouth
twist	meyer lemon

Method:

Pour the vermouth into a shaker over a handful of ice, stir or swirl* the shaker to allow the vermouth to coat and kiss the ice.

❖

Tip the vermouth out, leaving just the ice in the shaker.

❖

Add the gin and stir/swirl for several seconds.

❖

Double strain into a martini glass, ideally chilled for at least an hour before serving.

❖

Serve with the twist of meyer lemon.

**If mixing in a glass shaker, stir with a spoon.
If mixing in a stainless cocktail shaker, swirl In order to achieve the perfect dilution.*

The Oyster Box
Umhlanga, South Africa

Standing majestically on Umhlanga's prestigious beachfront with direct beach access and sweeping views of the Indian Ocean, The Oyster Box is one of South Africa's most distinguished hotels. Accommodations include 86 individually-decorated rooms, suites and exquisite villas, each equipped with the latest state-of-the-art amenities. A magnificent double-storied presidential suite, with private access and lift, offers the ultimate in luxury.

Renowned for its hospitality, service and cuisine, you have an excellent choice of venues for wining, dining and relaxing. The casual Ocean Terrace serves pizza from a wood-fire oven, the finest fresh seafood, and an authentic curry buffet while fine dining in the Grill Room is legendary. The Palm Court serves a lavish, traditional High Tea with live piano music daily. The Oyster and Lighthouse Bars overlooking the ocean and iconic lighthouse are the hottest spots in this charming seaside resort town.

Reflecting and celebrating the intricate tapestry of KwaZulu-Natal's rich Colonial-Afro-Indian culture, the award-winning spa's dedicated, trained staff delivers the highest levels of therapy and pampering. With six modern treatment rooms, a hydrotherapy bath, grooming lounge, plunge pool, state-of-the-art private gym, infinity pool, and post-treatment tranquillity lounge, you are totally pampered. The Spa also houses South Africa's only Hammam, an experience as special, as it is healing.

www.oysterboxhotel.com | Tel: +27 31 514 5000

About Umhlanga Schling...

The Oyster Box's signature cocktail is based upon the famous Singapore Sling served at the Long Bar in the Raffles Hotel in Singapore. This version uses local ingredients for which the east coast of KwaZulu-Natal is famous. Created by the hotel's mixologists for the re-opening of the hotel in 2009, you can enjoy this bespoke cocktail in one of hotel's stylish bars.

Umhlanga Schling

1.7 oz | 50 ml	mainstay cane*
0.8 oz | 25 ml	sugar syrup
2.5 oz | 75 ml	mango Juice
12 in | 30 cm	sugar cane
4	pineapple pieces
12	mint leaves

Method:

To the shaker add the cane spirit, sugar syrup, two slices of crushed pineapple and shake hard for 10 seconds.

Add the mint, clapped between your hands — not crushed — to just release the aromas and prevent it from going bitter.

Place crushed ice in a cyclone hurricane glass so it is 3/4 full, add the mixture, and stir clockwise for 10 seconds.

Add enough crushed ice to almost fill the glass and top up with mango juice.

Garnish with sugar cane and a pineapple wedge on the rim.

APPETIZER

Pimm's Cured Salmon

page 138

*A popular South African spirit. Available in shops and online.

Tenaya Lodge at Yosemite
Fish Camp, California, USA

Tenaya Lodge at Yosemite is a majestic Sierra resort set near the national park's soaring South Gate. As you turn off Highway 41 and enter the Tenaya realm, time brakes and senses awaken, hinting at the experience to come. Here, you have free rein to create an adventure all your own.

The Four Diamond, all-season resort offers luxurious lodging; recreation ranging from hiking, biking and swimming to skating and skiing; pampering at the Double Silver LEED-certified Ascent Spa; and a variety of onsite dining options ranging from casual to candlelit... all culminating with the chance to enjoy the lodge's signature "roughing it minus the rough part" approach to hospitality.

The inviting Jackalope's Bar & Grill beckons you to relax after a day of exploring with delectable, hearty choices that go well beyond classic pub fare. This laidback setting features rich hardwood floors, relaxing chairs and tables, a rough-hewn rustic wood bar, and Sierra-inspired photography – not to mention its famous horned hare mascot presiding over the comings and goings of guests. In addition to made-to-order fare like burgers, sandwiches, and specialty salads—many of which source organic and sustainable ingredients—Jackalope's boasts large selections of beer, wine, spirits and cocktails with local inspiration. From the outdoor fire pit and majestic views to the span of HDTVs for game day, you create your own agenda at Jackalope's.

TenayaLodge.com | Tel: +1 800 722 8584

High Sierra Bloody Mary

2 oz | 60 ml	Grey Goose vodka
6 oz | 177 ml	pre-made High Sierra Bloody Mary Mix*
1	lemon wedge
1	lime wedge
1	skewer with 1 gherkin pickle, green olive, banana wax pepper**, and cocktail onion

Method:

Salt the rim of a 22 oz glass.

❖

Fill glass with ice.

❖

Add vodka and premade High Sierra Bloody Mary Mix.

❖

Place celery, carrot, pickled asparagus and green onion in glass.

❖

Mix well.

For recipe, see Cocktail Essentials.
**A medium-sized chili pepper with a mild, tangy taste. Also known as the yellow wax pepper or banana chili.*

Four Seasons Safari Lodge
Serengeti, Tanzania

The 77-room Four Seasons Safari Lodge Serengeti, opened in December 2012, is particularly well-suited for first-time safari travelers, extended families and groups who appreciate luxury comfort as well as adventure. It includes 12 suites with plunge pools, five free-standing villas with private swimming pools, a spa with six treatment pavilions, three restaurants including the Maji Bar and Terrace with sweeping panoramas of the Serengeti, a Kijana Klub for kids as young as 2 years old to teens, and meeting facilities.

The two active watering holes on the property allow for magnificent animal viewing at peak times of day, and every room has an elevated open-air sundeck providing direct views over the Serengeti. Four Seasons Safari Lodge is also home to its own Discovery Center featuring museum-quality exhibits and a lecture hall for guests to learn about the local environment, wildlife and treasured Maasai culture.

Dining features local specialties as well as the freshest locally-sourced ingredients. You also drink in sweeping views at the Maji Bar and Terrace, known for its refreshing cocktails and delectable light fare including African tapas platters as well as comfort foods such as homemade pizza, pasta, sandwiches, burgers, and fresh organic salads.

www.fourseasons.com/serengeti | Tel: +255 768 981 981

About The Smashing Pumpkins Cocktail...

This specialty features five premium ingredients found within a 100-mile radius of the National Park. It all begins with pumpkins and lemons grown by Ikoma Cooperative Farms, a local purveyor. Additional ingredients include honey produced in the nearby village of Mugumu and Konyagi, a sugarcane-based spirit handcrafted in the city of Mwanza which gives the drink body. The recipe concludes on Lake Victoria where the final ingredient of fresh cinnamon powder is added for a spirited finish.

Smashing Pumpkins

2.5 oz | 70 ml	Konyagi liquor
2.75 oz | 80 ml	pumpkin purée*
1.5 oz | 40 ml	sour mix
1 pinch	cinnamon powder
	soda water

Method:

Shake all ingredients in a cocktail shaker with ice.

❖

Pour into a highball glass filled with ice cubes and top with soda water.

*See Appetizer Essentials for recipe.

Laucala Island, Fiji

Toucan Hill
Mustique, Grenadine Islands, Caribbean

In 1958, the island of Mustique, a hundred miles west of Barbados, was purchased by The Honourable Colin Tennant who presented a 10-acre plot to Princess Margaret as a wedding gift in 1960. In 1969, the 1,400-acre (5.7 km2) island was opened to outsiders willing to preserve the island's original environment, and the airport was opened. One of the most exclusive secure private islands in the world today, Mustique has retained its privacy, protecting the peaceful way of life paramount to all who live and vacation there including the Prince William, Kate and the Middleton family in 2013.

Atop the highest hill on the island rests Toucan Hill, an exquisite seven-acre Moroccan palace estate with 360° views of the Atlantic and Caribbean. Complete with elegant colonnades, courtyard gardens, mosaic tiled fountains, domed dining pavilion, and two infinity pools, this Moorish villa sparkles as one of the most elegant and spacious residences on Mustique. The four luxurious suites — "Toucan", "Sultan", "Pasha" and "Palm"— each have private terraces and balconies, king-size beds, large dressing rooms and tiled bathrooms. Touches of Moorish architecture are found in the ceilings and hanging lanterns. There's also the "Master Suite" that is only available on very limited occasions.

The culinary delights at Toucan Hill feature the freshest produce and seafood which helps support local farms and fishermen. The Villa manager can arrange picnics on the beach, or if you prefer, you can take your own vehicle and find a secret hideaway... or you can dine in the pavilion and watch the sun dance upon the sea during the day and moon sparkle upon the waters under the starlit sky.

www.toucanhill.com | Tel: +1 302 655 2882 (U.S.) or +1 784 488 8796 (direct)

Caribbean Pink Passion

1 lb | 0.45 kg	sorrel sepals (petals)
1.5 tsp | 7.5 g	fresh grated ginger
5 tbsp | 75 g	sugar
2.11 qts | 2 liters	water
splash	rum
twist	lemon, lime or orange

Method:

Put the ginger, sorrel and water in a large sauce pan and bring to a boil for 10 minutes. Remove from the heat.

Once mixture has cooled, place in refrigerator for 24 hours.

Remove from fridge and strain.

Stir in the sugar and a dash of rum. (The rum helps to preserve the drink.)

Optional: You can add some sherry or additional rum at this stage.

Serve with ice and garnish with a twist of lime, lemon or orange.

APPETIZER
Curry Coconut Shrimp with Pineapple & Caramelized Leeks
page 147

SIGNATURE COCKTAILS & APPETIZERS *from* AROUND THE WORLD

Condado Plaza Hilton
San Juan, Puerto Rico

Located on San Juan's sophisticated Condado strip just 10 minutes from the heart of the island's capital, the Condado Plaza Hilton has the distinction of being the only hotel to overlook both the Atlantic Ocean and tranquil Condado Lagoon. Designed by renowned architect Morris Lapidus in 1963, the landmark property features 571 deluxe guest rooms and suites recently renovated by noted designer Leo Daly to offer sleek contemporary interiors, many with private balconies and breathtaking water views. The nine restaurants, bars and lounges – including the flagship restaurant of top Puerto Rican Chef Wilo Benet – pleases every taste and style.

In the hotel's lobby, Ashford Sports Lounge offers guests and locals a modern, refined atmosphere for sports competitions complemented by a distinct menu featuring creative cocktails, craft beers and flavorful fare. Also available are a private beach and protected swimming area, three outdoor swimming pools, tennis courts, 24-hour fitness center, ScoutAbout children's activity program, 24-hour 12,500 square-foot casino, and 40,000 square feet of meeting space. The hotel's sleek design makes it the ideal urban retreat for business or leisure travel with a cosmopolitan sophistication blending with San Juan's colonial tradition.

The sunny days are also perfect for exploring the coast on a SUP (stand-up paddleboard), kayaking through the tranquil lagoon, and discovering the underwater indigenous-themed reef at the protected beach. You'll also want to stroll the historic streets of Old San Juan and enjoy its vibrant nightlife.

www.condadoplaza.com | Tel: +1 787 721 1000

Mojito Caribe Frozen

1 oz	30 ml	coco rum
1 oz	30 ml	mint
2 tsp	10 ml	lemon
0.5 oz	15 ml	passoã rum
8 oz	227 g	ice

Method:

Mix the coco rum, mint and lemon in a blender.

❖

Add ice and blend until frothy.

❖

Pour into a chilled margarita glass.

❖

Finish with the passoã rum and a sprig of mint on top.

Tequila Grilled Shrimp Shooter — APPETIZER
page 119

Hôtel Le Toiny
Saint Barthélemy, French West Indies

A chic 5-star Relais et Châteaux Island resort comprised of 15 luxurious villa suites in a sumptuous tropical setting with views of the ocean and Toiny Bay, Hôtel Le Toiny invites you to experience the island and hotel with its famous French fine-dining restaurant. Situated around 42 acres of lush tropical gardens, it is pure paradise in the hills of St. Barth.

Each accommodation is placed individually amid dense tropical vegetation and has its own private pool and panoramic views of the bay and Caribbean. La Villa, the largest suite, is comprised of a 1215 sq. ft. (110 m2) master villa with vaulted ceilings and hardwood floors. Included are a large living room, a kitchen corner, bedroom with en suite bathroom, and bay windows opening onto an expansive terrace overlooking the sea and secluded private pool. It also has two one-bedroom cottages with their own terraces and ocean views. Amenities include air conditioning, mini bar, TV with VOD and satellite, and WIFI access. Hammocks, beach chairs and coolers are also available on request.

Hôtel Le Toiny's St. Barth Restaurant offers one of the best French culinary experiences in the islands. Overseen by Chef Jean-Christophe Gille, the menu features the freshest seafood, poultry and other local ingredients as well as beef, French cheeses and a fine wine list.

www.letoiny.com | Tel: +590 590 27 88 88

Cobana Cocktail

1 oz	30 ml	cachaça*
0.7 oz	21 ml	coconut liqueur
1.4 oz	42 ml	coconut water
1.4 oz	42 ml	coconut milk
2.8 oz	83 ml	banana nectar

Method:

Mix well all the ingredients in a chilled shaker.

Fill the coconut glass with ice cubes and add the cocktail.

Decorate with coconut shavings and add a straw.

APPETIZER

Carpaccio & Ceviche of Mahi Mahi

page 133

*A Brazilian distilled spirit made from sugar cane juice. Also known as aguardente, pinga, and caninha.

Scrub Island Resort, Spa & Marina
Scrub Island, British Virgin Islands

The award-winning Scrub Island Resort, Spa & Marina, named after its location, is a serene 230-acre private-island haven at the east end of Tortola in the British Virgin Islands. The first member of Marriott's Autograph Collection in the Caribbean, the boutique resort is tucked into a rugged cliff overlooking the Atlantic, Caribbean, and neighboring uninhabited islands.

Here, laid-back Caribbean lifestyle meets the pleasures of the modern world. There are 26 ocean-view guest rooms and 26 ocean-view one-bedroom suites plus two-, three-, and four-bedroom luxury villas. The rich Caribbean woods and vibrant colors are complemented by amenities including king-size beds, luxurious Egyptian combed cotton linens,

plasma TVs, bamboo ceiling fans, air conditioning, bathrooms with separate shower and bathtub, and complimentary WiFi access.

Honored as a Top 10 Spa by *Caribbean Travel & Life*, the Ixora Spa experience is enhanced by its stunning hillside setting overlooking the crystal clear Caribbean waters. The resort is also home to the newest marina in the British Virgin Islands where most of the water activities begin including sea kayaking, stand up paddle boarding, snorkel tours, dive trips, sightseeing charters, speed boating, island hopping, sailing cruises and more. Located in the heart of the resort, the marina is a short stroll away from the variety of bars, restaurants and shops in Marina Village.

www.scrubisland.com | Tel: +1 877 890 7444 (toll free from US & Canada)
+1 813 849 4100 (from other areas)

Scrub Island Flirt

0.5 oz | 15 ml	simple syrup
1.5 oz | 45 ml	Pusser's dark rum
1 oz | 30 ml	peach purée*
2 slices	cucumber
splash	orange juice

Method:

Muddle cucumber and add all remaining ingredients in a shaker.

❖

Shake vigorously for five seconds.

❖

Pour over ice.

❖

Garnish with orange and cucumber slices.

See Cocktail Essentials for homemade recipe.

South Seas Island Resort
Captiva, Florida, USA

Seemingly set adrift off the Florida Gulf Coast, South Seas Island Resort is an unspoiled haven encompassing a wildlife preserve and two-and-half miles of shell-strewn beaches, lapped by turquoise tides. Recently recognized by MSNBC as a "Top 10 Best Place in the World to Experience Local Wildlife," South Seas Island Resort is set on 330 unspoiled acres with a rich variety of wildlife and boundless opportunity for adventure and relaxation.

The resort boasts a "Family, Nature, Comfort" approach to hospitality, attracting generations of families who have made the resort village their destination of choice for sharing treasured moments and making lasting memories.

The newest addition to South Seas, the Crooked Snook Tiki Bar, is nestled between the resort's pool and the Gulf of Mexico's seawall. The resort offers a variety of accommodations including villas, condominiums, cottages and homes.

You also enjoy world-class shelling along the beach, golf on a 9-hole executive course, the H2Whoa! Water Slides, an engaging ScoutAbout exploration program for families, and a list of family-oriented water sports, activities and interactive educational programs through the Sanibel Sea School. Ideal for events, this resort features a variety of venues and over 31,000 square feet of flexible function space.

www.southseas.com | Tel: +1 800 533 5553

Captiva Cooler

1 oz | 30 ml	pineapple rum
0.25 oz | 7.5 ml	banana liqueur
0.25 oz | 7.5 ml	mango purée
	lemonade
	cherry juice

Method:
Mix together rum, banana liqueur and mango purée and pour over ice.

❖

Top with lemonade and a splash of cherry juice.

APPETIZER

Half Jerked Chicken

page 153

Laucala Island
Fiji

"Bau nanuma na nodatou Lasa" or "Beautiful moments that last for eternity" Is an expression from an old Fijian folksong which is one of the core mottos of Laucala Island. Here is a paradise lost where anything is possible from a round of golf, cycling the island, game fishing, surfing, diving or sailing the turquoise waters or being pampered in the spa.

Each of the twenty-five villas widely spaced around the northern tip of the island has its own swimming pool and space for ultimate privacy. Seamless transitions from indoor to outdoor living create a relaxed yet luxurious atmosphere. Laucala also values its holistic approach to self-sustainability by growing all fruits and vegetables on its own farms, breeding poultry and cattle, making its own honey, baking its own breads, and bottling the purest volcanic mineral water to provide the best quality produce for its four restaurants.

You can experience 'cuisine à la Laucala' in the colonial Plantation House Restaurant, Asian-influenced dining in the tree tops of the Seagrass Lounge, spectacular sundown cocktails in the Rock Lounge, avant-garde finger food at the Pool Bar, and light lunches at the Beach Bar.

www.laucala.com | Tel: +679 888077

Laucala Island Bars...

Plantation House Bar located in an original colonial-style mansion provides perfect pre and post dinner experiences with a large variety of cocktails, wine, champagne, digestives and cigars.

Rock Lounge offers scenic views overlooking Seagrass Bay with its spectacular sunsets as Joeli, the bar manager displays his talent in creating cocktails with the freshest island ingredients.

The Beach Bar offers a relaxed atmosphere where fine white sand, blue sunny skies, crystal clear waters and freshly caught fish come together creating the perfect beach setting.

Laucala Lagoon

1.5 oz | 45 ml	gin bombay sapphire
0.6 oz | 18 ml	blue curacao
0.5 oz | 15 ml	fresh lime juice
	homemade limeade*

Method:
Mix the gin, blue curacao and the fresh lime juice with ice in the shaker.

❖

Pour into a cocktail glass and top with lemonade.

APPETIZER
Coral Trout Ceviche
page 131

*Fresh lime juice, sparkling water and white sugar to taste.

Jade Mountain
St. Lucia, West Indies

Jade Mountain, rising above its sister resort Anse Chastanet 's 600 acres of beachfront on St. Lucia's southwestern coastline, is an extraordinary island paradise. Recognized in 2015 by *Travel + Leisure* as 'The Best Hotel in the Caribbean', this multi-award-winning hilltop property is pure tranquility with stunning views of the old French colonial town of Soufriere and Twin Pitons, both of which are part of a UNESCO World Heritage Site. Its 22 cantilevered suites, designed as sanctuaries with private pools, have panoramic views of the surrounding scenery instead of a fourth wall. The extraordinary architecture, conceived and built by visionary owner Nick Troubetzkoy, is in perfect harmony with its natural surroundings.

Enveloped by an infinity pool, dining on a private hillside terrace in the Jade Mountain Club also offers panoramas from every table. Exclusively for resident guests, its Jade Cuisine, created by James Beard Award winner Chef Allen Susser, is a fusion of tropical, cultural and Caribbean flavors reflective of seasonal changes. On select evenings, you'll also enjoy entertainment ranging from local jazz musicians to acoustic guitarists.

There is also a wide range of spa services to be enjoyed in your sanctuary or at Kai en Ciel, the boutique spa and fitness studio. You can also explore Jade Mountain's sister resort Anse Chastanet's restaurants, bars, boutiques, art gallery, spa, scuba, bike and water sports facilities as well as enjoy the soft sand beaches accessible by foot or a resort shuttle.

www.jademountain.com | Tel: from U.S. +1 800 223 1108 or +1 758 719 7365 (direct);
Tel: from the U.K. + 0800 141 2859 (toll free) or +01 189 089 995 (direct);
Tel: direct from other locales +1 758 459 7000.

About Stairway to Heaven...

Served at both Jade Mountain and Anse Chastanet, this cocktail was created by co-owner Karolin Troubetzkoy and was awarded the gold medal in a local competition. She thought the name was a perfect complement for resort's setting and admits to being influenced by the song.

Stairway to Heaven

1 oz | 35 ml	**Seventh Heaven ginger & Bois Bandé rum***
0.5 oz | 15 ml	**coconut cream**
1 oz | 30 ml	**orange juice**
1 oz | 30 ml	**bounty rum**
	pineapple wedge for garnish

Method:

In a blender, add the ginger & Bois Bandé rum, bounty rum, orange juice, coconut cream and crushed ice. Blend until frothy.

❖

Serve in a cocktail glass and garnish with pineapple wedge and cocktail parasol.

APPETIZER
Spicy Calamari with fresh Ginger
page 149

*Available in liquor stores and online.

SIGNATURE COCKTAILS & APPETIZERS *from* AROUND THE WORLD

The BodyHoliday
St. Lucia, West Indies

Set on a private cove on Cariblue beach in the northwest corner of Saint Lucia is The BodyHoliday, one of the island's foremost luxury resorts. The all-inclusive five-star property provides luxury accommodations, personalized service, five restaurants and bars catering to every taste in food and drink, a Wellness Centre, and full menu of activities.

Accolades for this widely-acclaimed property include the Wellness Centre being voted one of the best spas in St. Lucia and The BodyHoliday named one of the top all-inclusive resorts in the world. TAO restaurant was also voted by *Condé Nast* as one of the top 60 tables in the world. Based on the four key pillars of relaxation, restorative beauty, skin care clinic, exercise and good diet, The BodyHoliday offers everything from archery to scuba diving, spinning and Pilates to Ayurvedic treatments, Reiki and daily spa treatments as well as golf, tennis, fencing, archery, yoga, tai chi, aerobics, fitness and dance classes. Everything is included — all meals, wines with lunch and dinner, most bar cocktails, and evening entertainment.

The Piano Bar is almost a step back in time. A comfortable and relaxing, beautifully decorated nightspot, it stays open until the last guest retires. The white baby grand piano is a magnet for the would-be Frank Sinatra or Shirley Bassey as the pianist entertains you with his selection of songs — or yours.

www.thebodyholiday.com |
Tel: from US & Canada: +1 800 544 2883 or +1 973 940 0441; Tel: from UK & Europe: +44 (0) 203 096 1605; Tel: direct +1 758 457 7800

Lemon Rose Cocktail

2	lemon grass stems (chopped)
2	2 rosemary stems (chopped)
2	lime wedges
0.5 oz | 15 ml	ginger syrup
2.5 oz | 75 ml	gin
2 dashes	Angostura bitters

Method:

Add the lemon grass, rosemary, and lime to shaker then muddle for 10 seconds.

❖

Add the ginger syrup, gin, Angostura bitters and some ice.

❖

Shake and strain in martini glass. Garnish with lime.

APPETIZER

Lemongrass Shrimp Skewers

page 115

SIGNATURE COCKTAILS & APPETIZERS *from* AROUND THE WORLD

Velas Vallarta, Puerto Vallarta, Mexico

El Conquistador Resort & Las Casitas Village
Fajardo, Puerto Rico

Dramatically set atop a 300-foot bluff on the eastern tip of Puerto Rico, El Conquistador Resort & Las Casitas Village— a Waldorf Astoria Resort— spread across 500 acres overlooking the converging waters of the Caribbean Sea and the Atlantic Ocean. Guestrooms and suites are divided into five villages, including Las Casitas Village, a separate luxury resort which features one-, two-, and three- bedroom style villas as well as 24 hour resort butler service.

The AAA Four Diamond resort presents 23 restaurants, bars and lounges, from gourmet to casual, many with ocean views, including the highly-rated Chops Steakhouse. Drake's Martini Bar features a pool table and an extensive bar menu encompassing everything from light appetizers, fine wines and premium spirits, to traditional cocktails and innovative concoctions. Las Olas Lounge, located halfway down the cliffside at the Olas level, offers spectacular ocean views.

The family-friendly resort also features Coquí Water Park, a state-of-the-art aquatic playground; Palomino Island, the resort's private island presenting an enclave of water sports and other recreational activities along white sand beaches; Waldorf Astoria Spa, and an Arthur Hills 18-hole golf course. The resort is home to the largest, most comprehensive meeting space in the Caribbean with over 100,000 square feet of flexible indoor and outdoor meeting and event space highlighted by ocean and El Yunque Rain Forest views.

www.elconresort.com | Tel: +1 888 543 1282

Sangria de Coco

2 oz | 60 ml	white wine
1 oz | 30 ml	Don Q coconut rum
1 oz | 30 ml	apple juice
1 oz | 30 ml	pineapple juice
0.75 oz | 22 ml	cream of coconut *(preferably Coco Lopez)*

Method:
Mix all ingredients in a blender and serve in a glass with ice.

❖

Garnish with pineapple or apple.

APPETIZER
Salmorejo de Jueyes
page 121

Hacienda Petac
Merida, Yucatan, Mexico

The owners of this gracious, 17th century Spanish colonial estate have restored it exquisitely, respecting its historical and cultural legacy. The original, exterior walls have been painstakingly preserved and the interiors in peach, terra cotta and cornflower blue recall its 400-year-old splendor. Colonial antiques and custom-designed furnishings add authentic charm and warmth. The sweet and attentive Mayan staff adds to the feeling of a luxurious, private home.

Hacienda Petac rests on 250 private acres in an ecological Reserve just outside the little village of Petac. The estate is covered with lush, tropical gardens and lawns with sculptures, fountains, waterfalls and a beautiful swimming pool. Accommodating 10 to 12 guests in five spacious bedrooms, you and your party have exclusive use of the hacienda for the entire week including use of the private spa and gym. Also included is a tour the colonial city of Merida's museums, monuments, parks, markets and shops.

Within easy reach are archeological zones highlighting Mayan art and culture including Uxmal and Chichen Itza. You may also enjoy an excursion to the crystal clear underwater pools of the Yucatan called cenotes. Or, you can take a boat trip through the Flamingo and Wildlife reserve at Celestun. Still waiting is a guided tour to the Mayan archeological sites. And for beach lovers, the Gulf Coast beckons with deserted beaches, adjacent mangroves and flamingo reserves.

www.haciendapetac.com | Tel: +52 999 911 2601

El Flamboyan

2 oz | 60 ml	100% agave tequila
0.75 oz | 22 ml	fresh squeezed lime juice
0.75 oz | 22 ml	Jamaica syrup*
2 dashes	Angostura bitters
	club soda

Method:
Add all ingredients *(except club soda)* to shaker, fill completely with ice and shake vigorously, strain into iced high ball glass.

❖

Top with club soda.

For recipe, see Cocktail Essentials.

APPETIZER

Bocadita de Res

page 155

About the El Flamboyan...
Hacienda Petac's signature cocktail was named for the flame trees that greet visitors upon entering the gates to the private estate.

Velas Vallarta
Puerto Vallarta, Mexico

Velas Vallarta, an all-inclusive family resort located on 10 acres of oceanfront with lush gardens, is just minutes from downtown Puerto Vallarta and within walking distance of Marina Vallarta Golf Course. Situated on the emerald waters of Banderas Bay, Velas Vallarta features 345 suites in three eight-storey buildings, a high-tech convention center that can accommodate up to 700, three swimming pools, a rejuvenating spa with spa cabins seaside, fitness center, multiple restaurants, and an inviting lounge with live music.

Nightly theme dinners and local specialties please the most discerning palate, and room service is available around the clock. Guests are invited to relax with a refreshing cocktail, margarita, cerveza or other beverage in the casual, open setting of the Alhambra Lobby Bar featuring live evening entertainment including Mariachi bands. During the day, you can choose from an exciting array of activities and events from making piñatas, jewelry and yoga on the jetty to Mexican fiestas and casino nights.

The recently renovated Kids' Club welcomes children under 13 with supervised activities such as treasure hunts and building sand castles to face painting and crafting with beads, allowing parents to indulge in a choice of exciting or relaxing pursuits like a round of golf, a variety of excursions or pampering at the spa.

www.velasvallarta.com | Tel: +1 888 407 4869

Cucumber & Habanero Chili Margarita

8 oz	237 ml	tequila
4 oz	118 ml	cointreau
2 oz	60 ml	simple syrup*
10		limes
1/2		cucumber
1/2		habanero chili
		tajin chili (to taste)
		salt (to taste)
4 cups	140 g	4 cups	140 g ice

Method:

Wash and disinfect all fresh ingredients.

❖

Peel the cucumber and remove the seeds.

❖

Cut the habanero chili in half and remove the seeds.

❖

Squeeze the limes to make a fresh juice.

❖

Mix the ingredients with ice and blend until forming a frozen drink.

❖

Rim four glasses with salt and tajin chili, fill with frozen margarita, and enjoy!

*For recipe, see Cocktail Essentials.

APPETIZER
Seafood Bruschetta
page 143

SIGNATURE COCKTAILS & APPETIZERS *from* AROUND THE WORLD

GRAND VELAS RIVIERA MAYA
PLAYA DEL CARMEN, RIVIERA MAYA, MEXICO

Set on 205 acres of pristine jungle and mangroves and with the finest white sand beach in the Riviera Maya, the AAA Five Diamond Grand Velas Riviera Maya is an ultra-luxury all-inclusive resort. You can choose from among three separate ambiances in this Leading Hotels of the World member including an adults only oceanfront, family-friendly ocean view, and a Zen-like tropical setting embraced by the flora and fauna of the Yucatan Peninsula's jungle.

The 491 beautifully-designed suites are exceptionally spacious with more than 1,100 square feet each — all with balconies and some with private plunge pools. All feature fully-stocked mini bars, plasma TVs, wireless Internet access, L'Occitane amenities, artisanal tequila and Nespresso machines.

The eight restaurants include five gourmet offerings presenting a culinary tour of Mexico, Europe and Asia. The resort features six bars boasting rooftop views—Sky Bar, Karaoke Bar, tech-savvy Koi Bar, Piano Bar, Sen Lin Bar, and Aqua Bar with views overlooking the turquoise waters. Other features include a 24-hour personal butler concierge, 24-hour room service, three swimming pools, two fitness centers, water sports, an innovative kids club and teens lounge, and business center. The resort has won numerous awards from *Travel + Leisure, Condé Nast Traveler, USA Today, Virtuoso, U.S. News & World Report* and Forbes.com.

www.rivieramaya.grandvelas.com | Tel: +1 877 418 2963

Mango Caribe

1.5 oz | 45 ml	tequila
1 oz | 30 ml	white wine
1 oz | 30 ml	orange liqueur
3 oz | 89 ml	orange juice
2 oz | 59 ml	mango concentrate or crushed mango
5	mint leaves
	chili powder to rim glass
	orange slice and dried red chili for garnish

Method:
Add the tequila, white wine, orange liqueur, orange juice, mango concentrate and mint leaves to the blender.

❖

Blend until smooth.

❖

Rim a short glass with chili powder.

❖

Serve the mixture on the rocks, garnished with a quarter slice of orange and dried red chili.

APPETIZER
Breaded Mussels
page 123

SIGNATURE COCKTAILS & APPETIZERS *from* AROUND THE WORLD

Matlali Hotel
Punta de Mita, Nayarit, Mexico

Situated in the rolling hills of La Cruz de Huanacaxtle and overlooking Mexico's Banderas Bay, this Preferred Hotel Group-affiliated luxury resort features 40 private villas with sweeping ocean and mountain views, a full-service Makawé Spa, the elegant Raixes Restaurant, and classic Eva Mandarina Beach Club.

Widely considered a local hotspot, Eva Mandarina Beach Club is a toes-in-the-sand establishment that offers a wide variety of Mexican delicacies from seafood ceviches and shrimp aguachiles to traditional tacos with the

local fresh catch of the day. Located ten minutes from the property and designed by renowned Guadalajara-based artist Abel Galvan, the Beach Club showcases bright and colorful design features ranging from yellow rubber ducks to vivid white bicycles adorning the walls. At night, Eva Mandarina transforms into a social hotspot where hotel guests and locals alike mix and mingle within the club's sun-orange walls and ivory furnishings. Steps away from Eva Mandarina guests will find the club's signature VW Beetle designed with a funky neon graffiti that symbolizes the atmosphere of Eva Mandarina – that of an authentic twist on modern Mexico.

The nearby fishing village of La Cruz offers resort guests an authentic snapshot of Mexico with weekly live music at the plaza and fish brought daily into the Mercado del Mar. You can also enjoy a wide range of activities including catamaran sailing, diving, surfing, snorkeling, and fishing.

www.matlali.com | Tel: +1 866 286 2108

Macho Margarita

1	red bell pepper
1.5 oz | 45 ml	tequila silver
1 oz | 30 ml	triple sec
0.25 oz | 7.5 ml	lime juice
1/4 slice	cucumber
1/4 slice	serrano pepper
1 oz | 30 ml	pineapple juice

Method:

Carefully cut off and save the top of the bell pepper. Remove all the seeds.

In a blender, put the serrano pepper, cucumber and pineapple. Blend and strain.

In a mixer glass, add the tequila, triple sec and lemon.

Add the juice from the blender and ice, shake hard and pour into a bell pepper.

APPETIZER

Shrimp Ceviche

page 137

SIGNATURE COCKTAILS & APPETIZERS *from* AROUND THE WORLD

Casa Velas
Puerto Vallarta, Mexico

A luxury all-inclusive boutique hotel and ocean club for adults only, Casa Velas is reminiscent of a Spanish hacienda nestled on the greens of Marina Vallarta's 18-hole golf course. The hotel features a private ocean club and is just minutes from the beach. It has received the AAA Four Diamond Award for hospitality seven times and has been in the top two in *TripAdvisor* for Puerto Vallarta since 2010.

Located five minutes from Puerto Vallarta Airport and just 15 from the popular downtown area, art galleries and "El Malecon" (the boardwalk), the hotel features 80 spacious suites, some with private pools and Jacuzzis. Spa Casa Velas encompasses treatment rooms for singles and couples, hydrotherapy area, garden-view fitness center equipped with state-of-the-art exercise equipment, and a beauty salon.

A novel service is a handbag bar where guests can enjoy use of a "loaner" designer handbag at no extra charge. Emiliano, the AAA Four Diamond rated a la carte fine dining restaurant, is in the hands of one of the area's leading chefs creating Mexican and international cuisine. In addition, you are invited to soak up the sun and sip on a poolside cocktail at Aqua Bar, boasting a variety of hand-made tropical cocktails. A true foodie experience, guests can enjoy dining privileges at the sister resort, Grand Velas Riviera Nayarit, with three gourmet specialty options.

www.hotelcasavelas.com | Tel: +1 877 418 3011

Passion Fruit Dry Martini

1 oz | 30 ml	passion fruit pulp
1.5 oz | 45 ml	Absolut Blue vodka
1 oz | 30 ml	cointreau (orange liqueur)
5 drops	white vermouth
3	drops fresh lime juice
6	ice cubes

Method:

Frost the rim of a chilled martini glass with powdered chili.

❖

In a cocktail shaker, add the ice cubes, vermouth, passion fruit pulp, vodka, cointreau and lime juice. Shake vigorously and pour contents into the martini glass.

❖

Garnish with a twist of lime.

APPETIZER

"Emiliano" Tuna with Avocado Aguachile

page 117

Hamanasi Adventure & Dive Resort
Hopkins Village, Stann Creek, Belize

Green Globe certified Hamanasi Adventure and Dive Resort is an intimate, boutique eco-resort located south of Hopkins Village in Southern Belize. This secluded coastal property, just steps from the Caribbean Sea, is surrounded by tropical flora on the finest stretch of beach in the country. Hamanasi specializes in romance, adventure and award-winning service, offering an ideal location with convenient access to numerous on and offshore adventures while also providing an authentic cultural experience.

Set amid 30 acres of coastline and littoral forest, the eco-chic Caribbean ambiance flows from the private accommodations and lush gardens to the

Singanga Restaurant and Great House. Hamanasi offers 13 freestanding tree houses, luxurious suites and spacious beachfront rooms, all featuring Belizean hardwood furniture, air conditioning, ceiling fans and private porches.

When you first arrive, the bartender will greet you with a delicious, tropical drink to get your holiday started on the right foot. The recently-expanded bar and lounge area invite guests to kick back with one another enjoying cocktails, a game of chess or simply the refreshing Caribbean breeze on the veranda. The diverse and talented bartenders of Mayan, Garifuna, Creole and East Indian descent will serve up a kaleidoscope of cocktails sure to lift the spirits.

www.hamanasi.com | Tel: +1 877 552 3483

Coco Rumba

1.5 oz | 45 ml	coconut rum
0.5 oz | 15 ml	vodka
3 oz | 90 ml	fresh pineapple juice
0.25 oz | 7.5 ml	fresh lime juice
0.25 oz | 7.5 ml	blue curaçao

Method:
Mix all ingredients then pour over ice.

Garnish with a slice of pineapple and maraschino cherry.

Grand Velas Riviera Nayarit
Nuevo Vallarta, Mexico

Grand Velas Riviera Nayarit, a member of the prestigious Leading Hotels of the World, enjoys a privileged natural setting with flowering, landscaped gardens beside a long stretch of pristine beach against a dramatic backdrop of the Sierra Madre mountains. The centerpiece of the gardens is a three-tiered infinity pool, a preferred spot for catching the legendary sunsets.

The AAA Five Diamond all-inclusive resort features 267 ocean-view suites, some with private plunge pools, and all with plasma TVs, wireless Internet access, fully-stocked mini bar, L'Occitane amenities and Nespresso

machines. Of the resort's five restaurants — three, serving French, Italian and Mexican gourmet cuisine — have received AAA Four Diamond awards for distinguished cuisine and presentation.

Boasting luscious libations and appetizing edibles, the Lobby Bar is a lively gathering place for cocktails and conversation. Guests relax and watch their favorite sporting events on TV or lounge on the charming outside terrace, with Karaoke every Saturday at 9 pm. There's a poolside Aqua Bar for guests to enjoy while soaking up the sun. The resort has won numerous awards from *Conde Nast Traveler, Travel + Leisure, TripAdvisor, U.S. News & World Report* and *Forbes*, which named it one of the Top Ten Coolest All-Inclusive Resorts in 2012.

www.vallarta.grandvelas.com | Tel: +1 877 418 2722

Basil Martini

3	fresh basil leaves
1.5 oz | 45 ml	premium vodka
1 dash	natural strawberry jam
1 dash	grenadine
0.5 oz | 15 ml	lemon juice

Method:

Combine 2 basil leaves and the other ingredients with ice in a cocktail shaker.

❖

Give it a short shake.

❖

Strain into a martini glass and garnish with the remaining basil leaf.

APPETIZER
Salad with Blackened Bluefin Tuna
page 161

SIGNATURE COCKTAILS & APPETIZERS *from* AROUND THE WORLD

The Singular Patagonia
Puerto Bories, Chile

Once a post-Victorian 1915 cold storage plant, today The Singular Patagonia is one of finest hotels in South America and has been named Chile's #1 hotel in *Trip Advisor's* 2013, 2014 and 2015 Travelers' Choice Awards. Formerly the epicenter of the sheep farming industry, the resort sits on nearly 30 acres of breathtaking land in Puerto Bories overlooking the Fjord of Last Hope.

Following a meticulous 10-year restoration by fourth generation relatives of the plant's original owners, this designated national landmark opened as a hotel in December 2011 with 57 rooms and suites providing every luxury. In one of the last great wilderness areas, the

region remains untamed and pristine. And to discover its marvels, over 20 different Patagonia excursions are offered for everyone from the armchair naturalist to thrill-seeker.

After a day of trekking in Torres del Paine National Park, challenging the fiord, or just exploring the region, you can enjoy the wellness spa and relax in the bar before the evening's five-star dining experience. Chef Pasqualetto, who honed his skills in France, has spent the last 13 years in Chile perfecting his own unique style putting imaginative twists on dishes incorporating the freshest local ingredients.

www.thesingular.com | Tel: +56 61 2722 030

Rhubarb Sour

2 oz | 60 ml	rhubarb liquor
1 oz | 30 ml	white rum
1 oz | 30 ml	lemon juice
1 oz | 30 ml	sugar syrup

Method:
Mix all ingredients in a cocktail shaker.

❖

Add 4 to 6 ice cubes.

❖

Cover and shake gently for about 10 seconds.

❖

Add a splash of cold water and pour directly into the glass.

Uniworld Boutique River Cruise Collection

Aqua Expeditions' Aqua Mekong
Cambodia & Viet Nam

Launched in October 2014, Aqua Expeditions' *Aqua Mekong* sails between Siem Reap, Cambodia and Saigon, Viet Nam and is the only five-star small luxury cruise ship traveling this stretch of the Mekong River. Brainchild of Italian-American entrepreneur Francesco Galli Zugaro who established the company in 2007, the Aqua Mekong was custom built to embody the aesthetics of a sophisticated five-star hotel accommodating 40 passengers in 20 design suites, each with panoramic floor-to-ceiling views. There's a full-service spa, fully-equipped gym, screening room, outdoor evening cinema, library, observation deck, and top deck river-facing pool.

Cuisine by Michelin-starred Bangkok chef David Thompson combines the culinary traditions of Mekong River culture with the freshest local ingredients from the markets of Saigon, Phnom Penh and Siem Reap. Daily excursions to temples, markets, villages and French colonial homes are escorted by the ship's expert private guides aboard the Aqua Mekong's four launch boats. Passengers also have the use of the ship's 10 on-board bicycles.

During the high-water season (July-November), you experience the full history and culture of Mekong life meeting Khmer farmers, Buddhist monks and entrepreneurs in Vietnam's markets. During the low water season (December-June), more time is spent exploring the Cambodian stretch of the Mekong and Tonle Sap River.

Founded eight years ago by Francesco Galli Zugaro, Aqua Expeditions, headquartered in Singapore, also has two custom-built, luxury cruise ships on the Amazon River in Peru — the 12-suite Aqua Amazon and 16-suite *Aria Amazon*.

www.aquaexpeditions.com | Tel: +1 866 603 3687

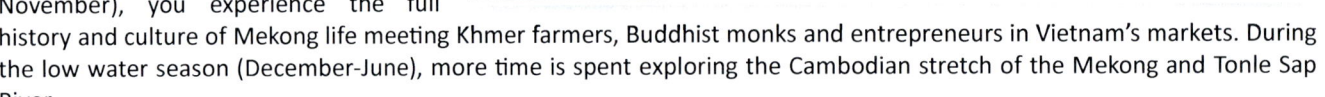

Kampot Fix

1.5 oz | 45 ml	ArteNOM 1580 tequila
0.5 oz | 15 ml	fresh squeezed pineapple juice
0.5 oz | 15 ml	fresh squeezed lime juice
0.5 oz | 15 ml	Kampot pepper syrup*
1 sprig	Thai basil

Method:
Combine all ingredients in a cocktail shaker with an ice cube.

❖

Shake and finely strain into a chilled cocktail glass.

❖

Garnish with fresh Kampot pepper and Thai basil.

*See Cocktail Essentials for recipe.

Uniworld Boutique River Cruise Collection
Europe, Russia, Egypt, India, China, Vietnam, & Cambodia

Uniworld's all-inclusive luxury river cruises take you right into the heart of the world's most fascinating cities, ancient towns and villages, grand castles, rolling vineyards, and each area's most important, intriguing historical treasures. Getting you there are unique floating boutique hotels meticulously designed with signature touches for which the company has earned numerous top accolades from *Condé Nast Traveler, Travel + Leisure, Saveur* and others.

Each vessel in the European fleet is one-of-a-kind with its own distinctive theme, original art, sumptuous furnishings and antiques. Stylish restaurants, plush lounges and full-service bars offer evening entertainment, dancing, or you can relax on the expansive deck, try out the well-equipped fitness center or indulge in a relaxing massage in the Serenity River Spa™.

With an average capacity of 130 guests, exclusive excursions, gourmet cuisine, and the highest staff-to-guest ratio in the river cruise industry, your onboard experience offers every luxury. You can choose from Vienna, Prague, St. Petersburg, Moscow, Vienna, Rome, Paris, Cairo, Beijing, Shanghai, Hong Kong, Ho Chi Minh City, Hanoi, New Delhi and dozens of other major and scenic destinations. For the fourth year running, *Travel + Leisure* named Uniworld the "Top River Cruise Line for Families" for its select summer departures in 2015. And for those who want to spend the holidays away from home, Uniworld's Holiday Cruises to Europe's most fascinating centuries' old Christmas markets are a popular option.

www.uniworld.com | Tel: +1 800 257 2407

Zorro Dry Martini

4.5 oz | 125 ml	gin
0.85 oz | 25 ml	fino sherry
2 dashes	Angostura bitters
2-3	green olive for garnish

Method:

Combine your favorite gin, a lovely Spanish dry fino sherry and 2 drops of Angostura bitters over ice in a cocktail shaker.

❖

Shake vigorously.

❖

Strain into a martini glass, garnishing with 2-3 olives infused with angostura bitters.

APPETIZER

Lobster Cocktail "Uniworld"

page 163

SIGNATURE COCKTAILS & APPETIZERS *from* AROUND THE WORLD

Jade Mountain, St. Lucia, West Indies

Appetizers

The BodyHoliday
St. Lucia, West Indies

INGREDIENTS

1	stalk lemongrass, woody ends trimmed and cut into 3 to 4 in | 7 to 10 cm skewers*
1	clove garlic, minced
1 tbsp | 15 ml	fish sauce
1 tsp | 5 ml	soy sauce
0.5 tsp | 2.5 g	ground chili paste
0.5 tsp | 2.5 g	ground black pepper
1 tsp | 5 g	St. Lucian honey
2 tsp | 10 ml	lime juice
2 tbsp | 30 ml	extra virgin olive oil
1 lb | 0.45 kg	medium to large raw shrimp - peeled, deveined, rinsed
0.5 cup | 68 g	dried coconut
4 tbsp | 60 ml	coconut cream
2 tsp | 10 g	baby cilantro
	finely-chopped scallions or mint
	St. Lucian fruit chutney as accompaniment

Lemon Grass Shrimp Skewers

SERVES: 4-6

METHOD

In a blender or food processor, combine the shrimp, garlic, fish sauce, soy sauce, chili paste, honey, lime juice, coconut oil, cilantro, black pepper and blend until smooth.

❖

Transfer shrimp mixture to a medium bowl. Let stand for 15 minutes.

❖

Mould the mixture around one end of each lemon grass skewer and refrigerate for 15-30 minutes.

❖

Remove from the fridge and roll the mixture on end of the skewers in the dried coconut.

❖

Toast the rest of the coconut.

❖

Preheat enough coconut oil in a small deep pan to vertically cover the mixture on the ends of the lemongrass.

❖

Lower the shrimp skewers into the oil with the wooden tops upright and out of the oil. Cook for a couple of minutes.

❖

Remove from heat and finish in a preheated 450°F | 232°C oven for three minutes or until cooked through.

TO ASSEMBLE

On individual appetizer plates, place two skewers sprinkled with scallions or mint.**

❖

Serve with the toasted dried coconut and fruit chutney -- preferably St. Lucian.

*Short bamboo or wooden skewers can be substituted if lemongrass is not available.
**Can also arrange on a serving platter.

Casa Velas
Puerto Vallarta, Mexico

INGREDIENTS

TUNA

1.6 oz | 45 g	fresh tuna
3.75 tsp | 18.5 g	Italian parsley
0.5 tbsp | 7.5 g	fresh thyme
4 tbsp | 60 g	dry chili seeds
5 oz | 148 ml	olive oil
	pinch salt
	pinch black pepper

AVOCADO AGUACHILE

2 oz | 60 ml	lemon juice
9 oz | 250 g	avocado pulp
0.5 tbsp | 7.5 g	fresh coriander
0.33 tbsp | 5 g	serrano chili
0.33 tsp | 1.6 g	salt
0.33 tbsp | 5 g	black pepper

GARNISH

3.3 tsp | 16.4 g	coriander sprouts
2.6 tsp | 13 g	roasted habanero chile
0.5 tsp | 2.5 g	red onion

"Emiliano" Tuna with Avocado Aguachile
(Mexican Ceviche)

SERVES: 1

METHOD

TUNA

Cut and shape tuna into two cubes of equal size.

Season tuna with salt and black pepper and a touch of olive oil,
then roll cubes over dry chili seeds mixed with finely chopped herbs,
encrusting all sides of the tuna.

Sear all sides of tuna in a pan for a couple of minutes. Let sit.

AVOCADO AGUACHILE

Blend the lemon juice, avocado pulp, fresh coriander, salt, black pepper and serrano chili.

Let sit for a few minutes for the flavors to unify.

TO ASSEMBLE

Put the avocado aguachile on part of the plate and place the tuna cubes on top.

Slice onion across and cut slices into quarters.

Julienne roasted habanero chili lengthwise.

Decorate the top with the coriander sprouts, and place the red onions
and roasted habanero in a miniature spoon to the side.

Condado Plaza Hilton
San Juan, Puerto Rico

INGREDIENTS

SHRIMP

12	large shrimp
1.5 oz | 45 ml	tequila
	pinch oregano
	salt and pepper to taste
	cocktail sauce*
	celery sticks
	carrot sticks
	fried plantains**

COCKTAIL SAUCE

0.5 cup | 118 ml	bottled chili sauce
1 tbsp | 15 g	horseradish
1 tbsp | 15 ml	lemon juice
2 tsp | 30 ml	Worcestershire sauce
	kosher salt
	fresh cracked black pepper

Tequila Grilled Shrimp Shooter

SERVES: 4-5

METHOD

SHRIMP

Mix first five ingredients in a bowl
and let sit for 15 minutes.

Cook shrimp at a medium-high temperature
on a pre-heated grill or grill pan.

Let cool.

COCKTAIL SAUCE

Combine all ingredients in a small bowl.

Mix well.

Cover and refrigerate for several hours.

TO ASSEMBLE

Place some chopped lettuce in a shot glass
and top with 2 tbsp | 30 ml cocktail sauce.

Add one shrimp, a celery stick, carrot stick
and fried plantain.

*Bottled can be substituted.
**See Appetizer Essentials for recipe.

El Conquistador Resort
Fajardo, Puerto Rico

INGREDIENTS

1 tbsp | 15 ml	extra virgin olive oil
0.25 cup | 40 g	diced onion
0.25 cup | 45 g	diced green pepper
0.25 cup | 45 g	diced red pepper
2 tbsp | 24 g	sofrito*
0.33 bottle	clam juice
2 tbsp | 30 ml	tomato sauce
10 oz | 473 g	land crab (juey)**
2	firm, ripe plantains

Salmorejo de Jueyes

(Stewed Land Crab)

SERVES: 4-5

METHOD

Dice the onions, green and red peppers into small cubes.

In a medium saucepan, heat the oil until fragrant.
Add the onions and peppers.
Stir to coat well, then lower the heat to medium.

Add sofrito and cook until tender.

Add the remaining ingredients and bring to a boil.

Lower the heat and simmer gently, uncovered, for about 30 minutes until thickened.

FRIED PLANTAIN

Blend the lemon juice, avocado pulp, fresh coriander, salt, black pepper and serrano chili.

Let sit for a few minutes for the flavors to unify.

Peel the plantains and cut each in half crosswise. Then cut each piece in half lengthwise.

Deep fry until they are floating.

Take the plantains out of the oil, drain and smash with a heavy iron skillet or mallet to flatten them on the cutting board without breaking them apart.

Return the flattened pieces to the oil and cook until crispy. Drain.

TO ASSEMBLE

Place three twice-fried plantains in a small dish.

Add a couple of tablespoons of the crab mixture over the top half of the plantains.

Garnish with a halved cherry tomato and fresh parsley or other herb.

For recipe, see Appetizer Essentials.
**Any other kind of available crab, preferably fresh, may be substituted.

GRAND VELAS RIVIERA MAYA
Playa del Carmen, Riviera Maya, Mexico

INGREDIENTS

MUSSELS

20	mussels
0.66 cup | 100 g	celery
0.75 cup + 1 tbsp | 100 g	leek
2 tbsp | 20 g	garlic
6.33 cup | 1.5 L	water
0.25 cup | 50 ml	white wine
0.25 cup | 50 ml	lime juice
0.25 tbsp | 5 g	salt
1 tbsp | 2 g	bay leaf
20	short, thin bamboo skewers
	oil for frying

FILLING

0.33 cup | 50 g	white onion
4.5 tbsp | 5 g	garlic
0.33 cup | 50 g	jalapeño chili
0.33 lb | 50 g	Valladolid sausage*
0.2 cup | 5 g	epazote**
0.10 lb | 50 g	pork lard***
1 cup | 100 g	goat cheese
1 cup | 100 g	ricotta cheese
1.33 tsp | 3 g	black pepper

EMULSION

0.33 cup | 50 g	habanero chili pepper
0.66 cup | 150 ml	mayonnaise
3.33 tbsp | 50 ml	soy sauce
0.66 cup | 100 g	white onion
1 cup | 30 g	fresh coriander

BREADING

2 cups + 2 tbsp | 200 g	wheat flour
2.75 cup | 250 g	dry breadcrumbs
4	eggs

Breaded Mussels

Stuffed with Ricotta and Sausage

SERVES: 10

METHOD

MUSSELS

Place all ingredients, except for the mussels, in a pot and bring to a boil.

❖

When reaching boiling point, add the mussels and cook for 8 minutes.

❖

Remove from heat. Take out the mussels and set aside.

FILLING

Finely chop the onion, garlic, jalapeño and Valladolid sausage.

❖

Chiffonade-cut the epazote.

❖

Melt the lard in a hot skillet. Add the onion and garlic and sauté for 2 minutes

❖

Add the sausage, jalapeño and epazote. Cook for 10 minutes then remove from the heat and drain out the excess fat.

❖

Let sit and cool, then mix with the remaining ingredients.

❖

Once you have readied the filling and mussels, stuff the filling into the mussels, then roll them through the flour, then in the egg and finally through breadcrumbs.

❖

The breaded mussels are now ready for frying over medium-high heat until golden brown on all sides.

EMULSION

Chop the onion and habanero and lightly sauté in a pan.

❖

Add soy sauce and blend in the remaining ingredients.

TO ASSEMBLE

Place the emulsion in the bottom of 10 small glass bowls.

❖

Skewer each mussel with a bamboo stick and stand up two in each bowl.

❖

Garnish with fresh herbs and fruit.

*Valladolid is Yucatan state's second city and known for its longaniza, a smoked sausage with local spices. It's hard to find the original, but versions of longaniza can be found in Latin markets and online.
**Epazote, common to Mexican cooking, is an herb with a slightly tangy flavor reminiscent of oregano. While fresh should be your first choice, you can substitute the dried herb, using one-half the amount specified for fresh leaves.
***If preferred, substitute an equal amount of vegetable shortening.

The Greenwich Hotel
New York City, New York USA

INGREDIENTS

GARLIC CREAM

1 tbsp | 15 ml	extra-virgin olive oil
2	cloves garlic, sliced thin
1 cup | 235 ml	heavy cream
	pinch salt
	pinch fresh-ground black pepper
	pinch cayenne pepper
6 oz | 170 g	lump crab meat

CRAB TOASTS

12 slices	ciabatta bread
1 tbsp | 15 ml	extra-virgin olive oil
1 cup | 236 g	medium zucchinis, cut in half lengthwise and sliced into thin moon shapes
	pinch salt
	pinch fresh-ground black pepper
9 oz | 255 g	can crushed tomatoes, well drained
1 half	jalapeño pepper, halved, seeds removed, and sliced thin

Locanda Verde's Crab Crostino

Created by Chef Andrew Carmellini

SERVES: 6

METHOD

GARLIC CREAM

Heat the olive oil in a medium saucepan over medium heat.

❖

Add the garlic and sauté, stirring constantly over medium heat for about 2 minutes, until the slices turn golden in the center and brown on the edges. The garlic will crisp up a bit, but don't let it burn.

❖

Add the heavy cream, turn up the heat to high for about 7 minutes. Let the cream boil until it's reduced to about 0.25 cup | 60 ml of a pretty thick cream.

❖

Add the salt, black pepper, and cayenne pepper. Stir everything together so it's well combined.

❖

Put the lump crab in a small bowl, pour the cream mixture over the top, and stir it completely into the crab.

❖

Check the seasoning. Add more salt, pepper, or cayenne if you think it is needed.

❖

Cover the bowl with plastic wrap and set it aside. Do not let it cool down.

CRAB TOASTS

Toast the bread so it's crisp and golden. You can also do this on a grill.

❖

Heat 1 tbsp | 15 ml of olive oil in a medium saucepan over medium-high heat.

❖

Add the zucchini slices and sauté for about 30 seconds until they are well coated in the oil. Season with the salt and pepper.

❖

Keep cooking the zucchini, tossing or stirring constantly, until it's just soft and the green color has intensified--about 90 seconds from the time it goes in the pan.

TO ASSEMBLE

Lay the toast out on a board. Spread each one with about 1 tbsp | 15 g of the crushed tomatoes.

❖

Put one spoonful of the crab mixture on top of each half so each piece has two evenly spaced mounds.

❖

Cut the toast in half, so each half has 1 lump of the crab mixture.

❖

Place 2 or 3 pieces of the zucchini on top of each crab mound. Add a slice or two of jalapeño and serve right away.

Hotel Casa 425
Ontario, California USA

INGREDIENTS

3 ears	yellow corn
2 oz | 60 ml	canola oil
1 tbsp | 15 ml	butter
3 tbsp | 45 ml	mayonnaise
4 tbsp | 60 ml	cotija cheese*
2 oz | 60 ml	chipotle peppers in adobo sauce, well blended**
0.25 cup | 12.5 g	cilantro leaves, chopped
1.5 tsp | 7.5 g	salt
0.75 tsp | 3.5 g black pepper	black pepper

Esquites (Roasted Corn Dip)

Created by Executive Chef Jordan Demere

SERVES: 2

METHOD

Shuck corn and cut from cob into a medium-size bowl.

❖

In a medium sauté pan, heat the oil and butter over medium-high heat until butter is melted.

❖

Add corn to pan and sauté, stirring occasionally until cooked and slightly browned on the edges.

❖

Remove from heat and return to the medium bowl.

❖

Add mayonnaise, 3 tbsp | 45 ml of the cotija cheese, the chipotle pepper,
3/4 of the cilantro leaves, salt and pepper. Mix thoroughly.

TO ASSEMBLE

Place corn mixture into a serving dish.

❖

Garnish with remaining cotija cheese and cilantro leaves.

❖

Serve with tortilla chips.

*A hard, crumbly, salty Hispanic-style cheese made from cow's milk. Well aged, cotija is similar in texture to crumbly goat cheese and is widely used on many dishes. Available in Latin markets and online.
**Cans available in Latin aisles of most grocery markets and online.
Before using, be sure to blend until the peppers, usually chipotles, are well minced.
Can be very spicy. Start with a small amount, increasing up to 2 oz | 60 g, tasting frequently.

The Lafayette Hotel Swim Club & Bungalows
San Diego, California USA

INGREDIENTS

3 slices	French baguette, 0.5 in | 12 mm thick
4 oz | 115 g	bay scallops (60-80 count)
1 tsp | 5 g	minced garlic
0.5 oz | 14 g	chopped cilantro
0.25 oz | 8 g	chopped walnuts
1 oz | 28 g	shredded parmesan cheese
3.3 oz | 90 g	diced plum tomatoes
2.5 oz | 75 ml	blended olive oil
0.5 oz | 15 ml	lemon oil
	pinch kosher salt
	pinch white pepper

Pacific Bay Scallop Bruschetta

Created by Executive Chef Ryan Gilbert

SERVES: 1

METHOD

In a food processor, combine the cilantro, garlic, walnuts, parmesan and pulse thoroughly until blended into a pesto. Slowly add 2 oz | 60 ml olive oil until emulsified.

❖

Brush baguette slices with some of the remaining olive oil on one side and brown on a hot griddle. Reserve remaining oil for scallops.

❖

Heat a small sauté pan over medium-high heat and add remaining olive oil. Add scallops and sauté for 2 minutes.

❖

Add the tomatoes and pesto. Sauté an additional minute.

❖

Season with salt and white pepper.

TO ASSEMBLE

Place the griddled baguette slices on a square or rectangular serving dish.

❖

Place a third of the scallop bruschetta on each slice of baguette.

❖

Top with remaining cilantro and walnuts.

❖

Garnish with fresh microgreens.

❖

Drizzle lemon oil around the plate and serve

Laucala Island
Fiji

INGREDIENTS

TROUT CEVICHE

7 oz | 200 g	coral trout fillet, skin removed	
1 tbsp | 15 g	red onion	
1 tbsp | 15 g	diced celery	
1 tbsp | 15 g	peeled tomato, diced	
1 tbsp | 15 g	diced cucumber	
1 tbsp | 15 g	diced pineapple	
1 tbsp | 15 g	diced avocado	
1 tbsp | 15 g	diced capsicum	
1 tbsp | 15 ml	coconut milk	
2 tbsp | 30 ml	lime juice	
1 tsp | 5 g	chili, diced, seeds removed	
1 tsp | 5 g	coriander	
1 tsp | 5 g	mint	

TOSTADAS

16 oz | 453 g	plain flour
pinch	salt
pinch	baking powder
2 oz | 59 g	pork lard
0.75 cup | 177 ml	warm water

Coral Trout Ceviche

SERVES: 4

METHOD

TOSTADAS

Mix flour, baking powder, salt and lard in a mixing bowl.

❖

Add warm water slowly until a smooth dough is formed.

❖

Rest for 20 minutes in fridge.

❖

Roll out to a thickness of 0.2 in | 5 mm.

❖

Cut out dough with a ring cutter 6 in | 15 cm in diameter.

❖

Fry at 355°F | 180°C until golden.

❖

Season with salt and espelette pepper powder* and serve with cerviche.

TROUT CEVICHE

Add lime juice to trout and soak for 2-3 minutes until the edges turn white.

❖

Add all the vegetables and mix thoroughly.

❖

Finish with fresh herbs, salt and coconut milk.

❖

Serve immediately.

TO ASSEMBLE

Place ceviche in a serving dish.

❖

Garnish with flat leaf parsley or other fresh herb.

Also known as a bell pepper
**A dark, slightly smoky pepper produced in France.
Available in specialty markets and online.

HÔTEL LE TOINY
SAINT BARTHÉLEMY, FRENCH WEST INDIES

INGREDIENTS

MAHI-MAHI

20 oz | 567 g	mahi-mahi fillet
3.5 oz | 100 g	sea salt
3	star anise
1	lime
1.75 oz | 50 g	red onion
3.5 oz | 104 ml	coconut milk

VEGETABLES

3.5 oz | 100 g	long turnip
1	small chioggia beetroot*
1.75 oz | 50 g	cooked red beetroot
1/2	green zucchini
1/2	yellow zucchini
1/2	carrot

OPTIONAL

8	caviar
1	capers
	fresh coconut

MARINADE

7 oz | 207 ml	white wine
1.75 oz | 52 ml	white vinegar
3	garlic cloves
1	bouquet garni**
1	pinch salt
0.33 oz | 10 g	fresh ginger
1	small sweet chili pepper
10	grains black pepper

Carpaccio and Ceviche of Mahi-Mahi

SERVES: 4

METHOD

FOR THE MARINADE

Boil the first five ingredients together.

Add the ginger, sweet chili and black pepper.

Mix well and allow to cool.

FOR THE VEGETABLES

Blanch the vegetables in salted boiling water for 10 seconds.

Cool and marinate for 2 hours, then drain.

MAHI-MAHI FILLET

Put the mahi-mahi in a blend of sea salt, crushed black pepper and star anise for 2 hours.

Rinse with clear water.

Cut half of the fillet into thin slices for the carpaccio.***

Cut the other half into small cubes for the ceviche and season with lime zests, chopped red onion and coconut milk.

TO ASSEMBLE

Creatively present your way. For example, you can decorate the platter with nasturtium leaves, coconut shavings, edible flowers, few drops of coconut milk, caviar, etc.
See photo for ideas and be directed by your imagination.

Serve chilled.

*Slices of red, bulbous chioggia beets or beetroots reveal a pattern of light-red and white rings. The unique color pattern and sweet taste make it a favorite for salads and side dishes. Available in most markets.
**A bouquet garni is a bundle of herbs such as a parsley stalks, sprigs of thyme, bay leaf bundled and tied firmly into a celery stalk or in a muslin bag to keep everything together.
***Very thinly sliced raw fish.

TOWER CLUB AT LEBUA
BANGKOK, THAILAND

INGREDIENTS

TACO FILLING

8	large tiger prawns (16-20 per lb | 0.5 kg)	
2 tsp | 4.5 g	paprika	
1 tsp | 1.8 g	dried oregano	
1 tsp | 1.5 g	thyme	
1 bunch	fresh coriander, chopped	
1 bunch	fresh cilantro	
1 tsp | 2 g	dry mustard seeds	
2 tsp | 12 g	sea salt	
1 tsp | 2.33 g	ground black pepper	
1 tsp | 2.33 g	onion powder	
1 tsp | 2.33 g	garlic powder	
1 tsp | 5 ml	brown sugar	
1 tsp | 6 g	tomato paste	
1	avocado, sliced lengthwise	
1	shallot, julienned	
1	red bell pepper, julienned	
1	head romaine lettuce, chopped	
1	lemon (juice only)	
3	tomatoes	
	chili powder to taste	
	additional black pepper to taste	

CORN TORTILLAS

1 cup | 130 g	corn flour
0.5 cup | 118 ml	water

Seafood Taco

SERVES: 2

TACO SHELLS

Blend the flour with the water until the dough forms – adding water slowly, not all at once.

❖

When the dough is finished, let rest for 20-30 minutes.

❖

Roll the dough into 4 balls.

❖

Stretch each ball into a round tortilla shape, and pan fry on both sides until lightly crisp.

❖

Fold each tortilla in half allowing for a flat bottom to enable it to stand up.

PRAWNS

Place the prawns in a medium-sized bowl.

❖

In another small bowl, combine the paprika, oregano, thyme, coriander, dry mustard seeds, sea salt, black pepper, onion powder, garlic powder and brown sugar.
Pour over the prawns to marinate for 1 hour.

❖

Sauté the prawns in the marinade with the shallot and red bell pepper.

❖

Add the tomato paste, lemon juice and one-half bunch of chopped coriander.

CHEF'S SPICY SAUCE

Blend the tomatoes in a blender and pass through a cheesecloth.

❖

Season with black pepper and chili powder to taste.

❖

Add the other half of the chopped coriander leaves.

TO ASSEMBLE

Add some chopped romaine lettuce, sautéed prawns and a slice of avocado to each tortilla.

❖

Sprinkle tops with dices of red bell pepper.

❖

Serve with the Chef's Spicy Sauce on side.

Matlali Hotel
Punta de Mita, Nayarit, Mexico

INGREDIENTS

21 oz | 600 g	shrimp peeled and deveined
11 oz | 300 g	tomatoes
7 oz | 200 g	onion
2 oz | 50 g	cilantro
10 oz | 296 ml	lemon juice
1.5 oz | 44 ml	olive oil
1	avocado
	salt and pepper to taste
	leafy greens for garnish

Shrimp Ceviche

SERVES: 4

Blanche shrimp in boiling water for about 1 minute, then shock in ice cold water.

❖

Strain when cooled.

❖

Cut shrimp into 1 in | 2.5 cm pieces and add to bowl.

❖

Add diced tomatoes, onions, and cilantro and mix.

❖

Add salt, pepper, lemon juice, olive oil, mix and chill for 1 hour.

TO ASSEMBLE

Place some leafy greens in a serving bowl.

❖

Top with the shrimp mixture and diced avocado.

The Oyster Box
Umhlanga, South Africa

INGREDIENTS

SALMON

1 10-12 oz | 283-340 g	side of salmon
0.5 cup | 115 g	cup salt
3 tbsp | 36 g	sugar
0.25 cup | 30 g	fresh dill finely chopped
0.25 cup | 60 ml	Pimm's aperitif
2 tbsp | 30 g	lemon juice
2 tbsp | 30 g	lemon zest
2 tbsp | 30 g	lime zest
2 tbsp | 30 g	orange zest

ACCOMPANIMENTS

2	fresh medium-sized beetroots or red beets
1	large radish or 2 small
0.42 cup | 100 g	peeled watermelon
0.42 cup | 100 g	fresh watercress
50 g	quinoa
1.5 cup | 355 ml	chicken broth
2	passion fruits
2	quail eggs
	black and white sesame seeds for coating
	olive oil

Pimm's Cured Salmon

SERVES: 4

METHOD

SALMON

Remove any tiny bones from the salmon using a clean pair of tweezers.

❖

Rinse, pat dry and lay the salmon skin side down on several large sheets of plastic wrap.

❖

In a mixing bowl, combine the sugar, salt, dill, vodka and lemon juice.

❖

Spread the mixture evenly over the flesh of the fish, pressing it down gently.

❖

Sprinkle the lemon, lime and orange zest evenly over the fish.

❖

Wrap the salmon tightly in the plastic and place skin side down on a large flat dish.

❖

Place something flat and large over the wrapped fish i.e. a few heavy cans to weigh down the surface. Refrigerate for 24 hours.

❖

Unwrap the salmon and rinse under cold water. Pat dry and cut diagonally into paper thin slices.

ACCOMPANIMENTS

BEETROOT
Boil beets or beetroots in salted water. Allow to cool, then peel and cube.

RADISH
Thinly slice and soak the radish in a mixture of ice and water for 10 minutes. Remove and pat dry.

WATERCRESS
Wash and pat dry fresh watercress.

❖

Toss in olive oil before serving.

WATERMELON
Peel and cube watermelon.

❖

Roll in black and white sesame seeds.

QUINOA
Boil quinoa in 1.5 cups | 2.76 ml of chicken stock for 12 minutes or until fully cooked.

❖

Strain and toss in olive oil.

❖

Season with salt and pepper to taste.

QUAIL EGGS
Soft boil two eggs.

❖

Remove and place in a dish of cold water to cool.

❖

Peel and slice in halves lengthwise.

GOAT CHEESE
Blend with finely crushed black pepper, salt and lemon juice.

❖

Using a teaspoon, form into small quenelles (egg shapes).

❖

Refrigerate for about 2 hours before serving.

PASSION FRUIT OIL
Warm 0.5 cup | 118 ml of olive oil. Remove from heat.

❖

Strain the flesh of two passion fruits through a sieve. Place the dried pulp into the warm oil and allow to infuse for 24 hours.

TO ASSEMBLE

On a large platter or wooden tray, place the fresh watercress and lime wedges along one side as a salad.

❖

Place the thinly-sliced salmon, quail eggs, scoops of goat cheese and quinoa around the remaining parts of the platter.

❖

Serve with a homemade horseradish mayonnaise** and fresh crispy bread.

*Beetroot, the bulbous red portion of the plant root, is also just referred to as a red beet. It was first cultivated by the Romans and, in the 19th century, became widely grown for its sugar.
**See Appetizer Essentials for recipe.

Palazzo Avino
Ravello, Italy

INGREDIENTS

1 king lobster, approximately 21 oz | 600 g

BREAD "PIZZAIOLA" STYLE

0.5 cup | 100 g	stale bread cut in small pieces
3.5 oz | 100 g	peeled plum tomatoes
2 tbsp | 30 g	fresh onions
1 tsp | 5 g	fresh garlic
0.5 tsp | 10 g	chives
0.4 tsp | 3 g	dry oregano
1.5 tbsp | 20 g	fresh basil
1 oz | 30 ml	extra virgin oil
	salt and pepper to taste

BUFFALO RICOTTA RAGU

5.5 oz | 150 g	violet eggplants
2 tsp | 10 g	garlic confit*
0.4 tsp | 5 g	fresh thyme
0.4 tsp | 5 g	marjoram
0.4 tsp | 5 g	ginger
pinch	lime zest
2 tsp | 10 g	brown sugar
1 tsp | 20 ml	extra virgin oil
2 tsp | 10 ml	soya sauce
	salt and pepper to taste

EGGPLANT CAVIAR

3.5 oz | 100 g	ricotta cheese
2 tbsp | 30 ml	cream
0.35 oz | 10 g	milk

King Lobster on Bread "Pizzaiola" Style

SERVES: 1

METHOD

LOBSTER

Cook in abundant salted water for about 5 minutes.

❖

Cool in water and ice, remove the shell and keep warm

BREAD "PIZZAIOLA" STYLE

In a big pan fry oil, onions and garlic.

❖

Add the tomatoes and all the aromatic ingredients and cook for around 20 minutes.

❖

Add the stale bread in small pieces and stir all the ingredients.

❖

Place in a preheated 355°F | 180°C oven for around 5 minutes.

EGGPLANT CAVIAR

In a big pan fry the eggplants.

❖

Wash and dress them with oil, thyme, marjoram and cook in the oven for 30 minutes at 300°F | 150°C.

❖

When done, scoop out the inside of the eggplant and stir it with the remaining ingredients.

❖

Divide into small dollops (like caviar).

BUFFALO RICOTTA RAGU

Mix all the ingredients and keep the mixture cold in the fridge.

KING LOBSTER SAUCE

Boil the shells, carrots, onions, tomatoes, lemon, thyme.

❖

Use for plate decoration only.

TO ASSEMBLE

On the bottom of the plate, spoon around a small swirl of king lobster sauce.

❖

Place Bread "Pizzaiola" Style on top.

❖

Lean the king lobster claw against part of the body on top of the Bread "Pizzaiola" Style.

❖

Finish the plate with the Eggplant Caviar, Buffalo Ricotta Ragu and an edible flower for decoration.

*For recipe, see Appetizer Essentials.

Velas Vallarta
Puerto Vallarta, Mexico

INGREDIENTS

0.25 lb | 100 g	cooked shrimp
0.25 lb | 100 g	cooked octopus
0.25 lb | 100 g	margarita scallops
1 cup | 150 g	tomatoes, diced
0.33 cup | 50 g	onion, chopped
2	garlic cloves
1	loaf baguette bread
	chopped basil to taste
	balsamic vinegar to taste
	olive oil to taste
	salt and pepper to taste
	grated parmesan cheese for topping

Seafood Bruschetta

SERVES: 4

METHOD

Cut into pieces the cooked shrimp, octopus and scallops. Put into a bowl.

Add the chopped tomato, onion and basil.

Season to taste with vinegar, olive oil, salt and pepper.

Cut bread into 12 slices and lightly toast in a pan smeared with raw garlic.

TO ASSEMBLE

Arrange all ingredients on top of the toasted slices.

Finish by adding finely-grated parmesan cheese.

Royal Blues Hotel
Deerfield Beach, Florida, USA

INGREDIENTS

12	sea scallops
1	whole cauliflower
1 cup | 200 g	carnaroli or arborio rice
1 cup | 225 ml	almond milk
0.25 cup | 29 g	almonds
2	shallots
	salt to taste
	freshly crushed white pepper to taste
3 cups | 0.7 L	vegetable stock
	grapeseed oil for sautéing
	assorted microgreens for decoration*

Diver Scallops with Carnaroli Risotto

(Dairy Free)

SERVES: 4

METHOD

RISOTTO

Thinly dice one shallot and sauté in grapeseed oil.

❖

Once the shallots have become translucent, add the rice and gently cook for a couple of minutes, stirring constantly.

❖

Add the vegetable stock to cover the rice. Reduce and keep cooking until the rice is al dente, stirring frequently.

Set rice mixture aside to cool.

CAULIFLOWER PURÉE

Clean the cauliflower and cut one half into small pieces

❖

Slice the second shallot.

❖

Place the shallots and cauliflower in a pan over medium heat and cook for 2 minutes.

❖

Cover with almond milk and cook until the cauliflower is tender.

❖

Place mixture in a food processor and mix until you reach a purée consistency.

CAULIFLOWER FOR PRESENTATION

Cut the flowers off the other half of the cauliflower.

❖

Blanch them for 2 minutes

SCALLOPS

Sauté the scallops for 2 minutes on each side.

❖

Add the blanched cauliflower flowers and mix together.

❖

While scallops are cooking, place the risotto back on medium heat, add the cauliflower purée and stir.

TO ASSEMBLE

Place the risotto and purée mixture on the bottom of the plate.

❖

Place the scallops on top and garnish with the sautéed cauliflower.

❖

Place some microgreens for decoration.

❖

Serve immediately.

Shoots of salad vegetables such as arugula, swiss chard, mustard, beetroot, etc., picked immediately after the leaves have appeared. Can substitute other small-leafed greens.

Toucan Hill
Mustique, Granadine Islands, Caribbean

INGREDIENTS

1 tbsp | 15 g	butter
1 tbsp | 15 ml	olive oil
4	leeks, white and green parts, cleaned and diced
3	cloves garlic, chopped
2 tbsp | 30 g	green curry paste
1.5 lbs | 0.69 kg	shrimp
1 cup | 237 ml	chicken stock
1 cup | 237 ml	coconut milk
0.5 cup | 90 g	diced pineapple from half of a fresh pineapple halved lengthwise.

Curry Coconut Shrimp

with Pineapple & Caramelized Leeks

SERVES: 4

METHOD

Place the butter and oil in a saucepan over medium heat.

Once the butter has melted, add the leeks.

Lower the heat to medium-low and cook the leeks for 15 minutes until golden and caramelized.

Add the garlic and curry paste to the pan. Sauté for 2 minutes.

Add shrimp and pineapple. Continue to cook for approximately 3 minutes.

Add chicken stock and coconut milk and simmer for an additional 2 minutes.

TO ASSEMBLE

Place shrimp mixture in the scooped-out halved pineapple.

Garnish with leeks and cilantro.

Jade Mountain
St. Lucia, West Indies

INGREDIENTS

2 tbsp | 16.8 ml	clarified butter
6	large green onions, minced
2	cloves garlic, minced
2 tbsp | 30 g	fresh ginger, minced
1 tbsp | 30 g	madras curry powder*
.25 tsp | 1.25 g	cayenne pepper
1 tsp | 5 g	sea salt
2	large sweet potato, peeled and diced
0.5 cup | 118 ml	ginger beer
0.5 cup | 118 ml	cold water
1 cup | 237 ml	coconut milk
1 lb | 0.45 kg	calamari rings and tentacles, well cleaned
1 cup | 175 g	diced pineapple
4	sprigs shadow beni**

Spicy Calamari with Fresh Ginger

SERVES: 4

METHOD

In a heavy sauce pan, warm the butter.

❖

Sauté the green onions, garlic and ginger for 2 minutes.

❖

Add the curry powder, cayenne and salt and sauté for another 2 minutes.

❖

Add the sweet potato, ginger beer, cold water, and coconut milk and continue cooking over medium heat for 15 minutes.

❖

Add the calamari and pineapple, then bring it back to a simmer for another 4-5 minutes until the calamari are cooked through.

TO ASSEMBLE

Place on a decorative plate and garnish with shadow beni or other baby herb.

madras curry powder tends to be a little hotter, spicier than other curry powders.

**Shadow beni, a leafy herb native to the West Indies and Central America, can be found in specialty stores or online. If not available, cilantro can be substituted.

QT Sydney
Sydney, Australia

INGREDIENTS

10	pre-baked vol-au-vent cases (or small puff pastry shells)
2 tbsp | 10 ml	lemon juice
8 oz | 250 g	crème fraiche
1 tbsp | 15 g	finely chopped fresh dill
3.5 oz | 100 g	house-cured ocean trout, diced
5	quail eggs
0.7 oz | 20 g	sterling caviar
	pepper to taste
	fresh dill sprigs for garnish

CURED OCEAN TROUT

1	side ocean trout, skin on
7 oz | 200 g	sugar
7 oz | 200 g	salt
4 tbsp | 60 g	coriander seeds
4 tbsp | 60 g	black peppercorns
0.5 tbsp | 7.5 g	ginger powder
	handful dill, roughly chopped
	handful cilantro, roughly chopped
	handful mint, roughly chopped

Bringing Back the "Vol-au-Vent"

SERVES: 5-10

METHOD

Combine crème fraiche, lemon juice and chopped dill in a bowl. Season with pepper.

❖

Place the quail eggs in a saucepan of boiling water for just over 2 minutes.

❖

Remove them with a slotted spoon and immediately run under cold water for a minute.

❖

Peel the eggs and halve them lengthwise.

CURED OCEAN TROUT

Toast the coriander seeds and black peppercorns until fragrant.

❖

Once cooled, lightly crush with a mortar and pestle.

❖

Combine crushed spices with sugar, salt, ginger and fresh herbs to complete curing mixture.

❖

In a tray, lay a generous layer of curing mix. Top with the ocean trout and then cover with another layer of the curing mix.

❖

Cover with plastic and leave to cure for 24 hours — no longer.

TO ASSEMBLE

Pipe a small amount of the seasoned crème fraiche into the vol-au-vents.

❖

Top with the diced cured ocean trout.

❖

Top each with one quail egg half and garnish with a generous dollop of caviar and sprig of dill.

South Seas Island Resort
Captiva, Florida, USA

INGREDIENTS

1/2	chicken
3	small tri-colored sweet bell peppers
1 oz | 28 g	Caribbean slaw*
2 oz | 57 g	jerk seasoning*
2 pieces	fried tostones*
3 pieces	ripe plantains, fried*
	Green onions for garnish

South Seas Half Jerked Chicken

SERVES: 1

METHOD

Put jerk seasoning in a bowl, add chicken, and massage it well into the meat,
making sure you get it underneath the skin.

❖

Cover and marinate for at least 6 hours, preferably overnight.

❖

To barbecue: light a barbecue and allow it to cool to a medium heat
(you should be able to hold your hand over the grill for 4 seconds without getting singed).

❖

Add the chicken and sear on both sides.

❖

Move the chicken to the edges of the barbecue, put the lid down,
and cook for about 25 minutes, turning occasionally, until the chicken is cooked through.

❖

Or to cook in the oven: preheat oven to 355°F | 180°C.

❖

Place chicken in a roasting tray, cover with foil,
and cook in the pre-heated oven for about an hour, until cooked through.

❖

Heat a griddle pan on a high heat and then sear the skin side until charred and crisp.

TO ASSEMBLE

Serve with two fried tostones, two fried plantains, three lightly charred sweet peppers, Caribbean slaw.

*See Appetizer Essentials for all four recipes.

Hacienda Petac
Merida, Yucatan, Mexico

INGREDIENTS

3 lbs | 1.36 kg	beef sirloin, diced into 0.05 in | 1.27 cm squares
1	red bell pepper, finely diced
1	serrano chile, finely diced
1	medium onion, finely diced
3	cloves garlic, finely diced
3 oz | 89 ml	freshly squeezed lime juice
1 tbsp | 15 ml	salsa inglesa (Worcestershire)
0.5 tbsp | 22 g	maggi seasoning*
2 tbsp | 30 ml	olive oil
12	corn tortillas, cut into 2.5 in | 6.35 cm circles**
1/2	red onion, thinly julienned
1 cup | 50 g	cilantro, finely chopped
2	limes - juice only
	corn oil for frying

Bocadita de Res

SERVES: 8-12

METHOD

Heat corn oil in a fry pan.
Cut out tortilla circles and fry on both sides until crispy.
Drain and set aside.

To pickle the onion, place red onion slices in bowl.
Cover with boiling water over and let sit 15 minutes.
Drain then add the juice of 1 lime, dash of salt. Mix well and set aside.

In another bowl, combine meat with 1.5 tbsp | 22 ml olive oil, juice of second lime,
Worcestershire, and maggi. Marinate for 10 minutes.

Meanwhile sauté bell pepper and onion in 0.5 tbsp | 7.5 ml olive oil until soft, about 15 minutes.

Add the garlic, meat and serrano. Stir well.
Continue cooking until meat is done, about 5 minutes.

TO ASSEMBLE

Place about a tablespoon of meat mixture on top of tortilla.

Top with pickled onion and finely chopped cilantro.

*a dark, vegetable protein-based seasoning sauce very similar to soy sauce. Available in Asian markets and online.
**For recipe, see Appetizer Essentials. Packaged corn tortillas may be substituted.

Chandler's Bar & Lounge at Cape Rey
Carlsbad, California, USA

INGREDIENTS

2	2 medium red beets
2	2 medium yellow beets
2	2 medium carrots

CURRIED CANDIED PECAN DIP

0.5 cup | 115 g	mayonnaise
0.5 cup | 115 g	Greek yogurt
2 tbsp | 30 g	madras curry
0.25 tsp | 1.25 g	cumin
0.25 tsp | 1.25 g	coriander
0.25 cup | 60 g	chopped candied pecans
	salt and pepper to taste

Beet Chip Crudité

with Curried Candied Pecan Dip

SERVES: 4

METHOD

Peel vegetables.

❖

Using the slice blade on a food processor or a mandolin,
slice beets and carrots very thin so they are almost transparent.

❖

Soak in Ice water and refrigerate for 2 hours so the vegetable slices become crisp.

❖

Remove from water dry on paper towels.

CURRIED CANDIED PECAN DIP

Mix first 6 ingredients in a bowl and add salt and pepper to taste.

TO ASSEMBLE

Place vegetables on a serving platter. Top with ribbons of carrots.

❖

Garnish with fresh herbs and greens.

❖

Serve with a bowl of the dip.

Blantyre
Lenox, Massachusetts, USA

INGREDIENTS

2	lobsters, 1.5 lbs | 680 g each
1	English cucumber
1	grapefruit
1	orange
1	lime
1 bunch	cilantro
1 cup | 237 ml	olive oil
0.5 cup | 85 g	golden quinoa
1.5 cups | 355 ml	water

Maine Lobster Golden Citrus Salad

Created by Executive Chef Arnaud Cotar

SERVES: 4

METHOD

Boil the lobsters for 8 minutes, drain, then ice down to chill.

❖

Remove the lobster meat from the shells, keeping claw and tail sections intact. Set aside.

❖

Cook the quinoa in 1.5 cups | 355 ml water, covered, until done. Keep at room temperature.

❖

Over a bowl to catch the juices, cut off the peels of the fruit down to the flesh.

❖

Cut the fruit segments away from the membranes,
making sure no pith, membranes or seeds remain.

❖

Reserve the fruit segments.

❖

Before discarding the membranes, squeeze over the juice bowl to collect any remaining juices.

❖

Cook and season the cooked quinoa with 2 tbsp | 30 ml olive oil
and 3 tbsp | 45 ml citrus juice – to taste.

❖

Peel and dice the cucumber. Add some to the quinoa mixture, to your liking.

❖

Adjust seasoning. Add salt and pepper to taste

❖

Make a dressing with 2 to 3 tbsp | 30 to 45 ml of the collected citrus juice.
Mix with double the amount of olive oil and chopped cilantro to your liking

TO ASSEMBLE

Shape the quinoa mixture into four round patties and place one in the center of each plate.

❖

Top with 1 claw and 1/2 tail for each serving.

❖

Place segments of each fruit around the quinoa. Drizzle with dressing.

Grand Velas Riviera Nayarit
Nuevo Vallarta, Mexico

INGREDIENTS

0.5 lb | 20 g   bluefin tuna steak*

TUNA SEASONING

2 tbsp | 13.8 g	paprika
1 tbsp | 4.3 g	oregano
1 tsp | 1.8 g	thyme
1.5 tsp | 2 g	cayenne pepper, to taste
0.5 tsp | 1.4 g	black pepper
0.5 tsp | 1.4 g	onion powder
0.5 tsp | 3 g	garlic powder
	kosher salt
	cooking spray

SALAD

1 cup | 50 g	tender greens
0.5 tbsp | 7 g	cucumber
dash	beet vinaigrette
1 tsp | 5 g	Boursin cheese
0.33 tsp | 1.5 g	walnut oil
0.33 tbsp | 2 g	ground pepper
pinch	salt
3	pistachio nuts, baked and ground
	spiced bread croutons**

BEET VINAIGRETTE

0.75 cup | 30 g	beets
	sugar to taste
	raspberry vinaigrette to taste
	olive oil to taste
	pepper to taste
	salt to taste

Salad with Blackened Bluefin Tuna
and Red Wine Sorbet

SERVES: 1

METHOD

VINAIGRETTE

Cook the beets with the sugar. Drain and grind.

❖

Mix in the raspberry vinaigrette, olive oil, pepper and salt to taste. Set aside to let flavors blend.

TUNA

Mix all ingredients (except cooking spray) together and store in an airtight container.

❖

Preheat barbecue grill to high.

❖

Coat all sides of the tuna steak with a thick coating of seasoning and press well into the flesh of the fish.

❖

Spray one side of the tuna with cooking spray.
Place sprayed side down on grill grate.
Close lid and cook 1-2 minutes.
Open lid, spray other side of fish and flip.
Cook 1-2 minutes more.
Tuna is finished when outside edges are cooked but middle is still rare.

SALAD

In a small bowl, combine the greens and cucumber with the beet vinaigrette, salt, pepper and walnut oil.

❖

Make a border for the salad by cutting a thin strip lengthwise from an unpeeled cucumber and fasten the strip with a colorful toothpick to make a ring. See photo.

TO ASSEMBLE

On a single-serving plate, put the greens over the boursin cheese in the cucumber ring. Add the spiced croutons over the top.

❖

Cut the tuna into two equal portions and place to the side on the platter.

❖

Finish with an elongated scoop of red wine sorbet over the pistachio dust.

❖

Garnish with some edible flowers.

*Yellowfin tuna may be substituted
**See Appetizer Essentials for recipe.

Uniworld Boutique River Cruise Collection
Europe, Russia, Egypt, India, China, Vietnam & Cambodia

INGREDIENTS

2.5 tbsp | 38 g	fresh lobster meat
2 tsp | 10 g	granny smith apple
1	lemon wedge
1	beet root slice
1 tbsp | 15 g	Sauce Marie Louise (ketchup, brandy, horseradish, mayonnaise)
	Worcestershire sauce
	fresh lemon juice
1 tsp | 5 g	iceberg lettuce
	English celery, peeled and julienned*
	watercress

Lobster Cocktail "Uniworld"

Created by Uniworld Culinary Director Master Chef Bernhard Zorn

SERVES: 1

METHOD

Thinly julienne the apple.

Take some crushed ice and pour in as much salt as needed to keep the water as icy as possible.

Add the apple slices and soak them for 3–4 hours so they become really crunchy and icy.

Marinate the lobster meat in a little bit of Worcestershire sauce, freshly squeezed lemon juice, salt and white pepper to taste.

For the iceberg lettuce, chiffonade** only the tender green leaves and keep the strips in ice and salt like the apples so it will also be very crunchy.

Prepare the Sauce Marie Louise by combining equal amounts of ketchup and mayonnaise, then adding the brandy and horseradish to taste.

Mix the lobster meat with a little of the Sauce Marie Louise to add flavor.

TO ASSEMBLE

In a stemmed appetizer glass, place some of the iceberg lettuce chiffonade.

Place the lobster meat on top.

Put a dollop of the Sauce Marie Louise on top of the lobster meat.

Garnish with the slice of beet root, some watercress or dill, the apples and the celery.

Finish with a lemon wedge cleaned of seeds and white pith.

Julienne is a knife technique for cutting vegetables and fruits into long, very thin strips resembling matchsticks.

**Chiffonade is a technique used for cutting herbs and leafy vegetables like lettuce into thin strips or ribbons. To chiffonade the lettuce, stack the leaves then roll them into a tube. Carefully cut across the ends of the tube with a sharp knife to make the fine strips.

W Scottsdale Hotel
Scottsdale, Arizona, USA

2 oz | 57 g	white balsamic dressing*
1 tbsp | 15 g	toasted coconut
3 oz | 85 g	diced pineapple
3 oz | 85 g	diced cantaloupe
3 oz | 85 g	diced honeydew melon
3 oz | 85 g	diced watermelon
3 oz | 85 g	diced kiwi
1 oz | 28 g	grapes
1 tsp | 5 g	fresh mint

Fruit Salad

SERVES: 1

TOASTED COCONUT

Preheat oven to 350°F | 188°C.

❖

Spread coconut around an ovenproof pan.

❖

Put pan on the center shelf of the oven and bake about 10 minutes or until flakes start to brown.

❖

Stir frequently so they brown evenly.

❖

Transfer flakes from the pan to a small plate. Let cool.

FRUIT

Wash all fruits thoroughly.

❖

Chop pineapple, cantaloupe, honeydew melon, kiwi, and watermelon into bite sized pieces.

TO ASSEMBLE

Combine diced fruit, grapes, toasted coconut, and white balsamic dressing in a salad bowl.

❖

Toss and mix salad.

❖

Garnish with fresh mint and serve.

See Appetizer Essentials for recipe.

Vecchia Glass Factory, Venice Italy

Cocktail Essentials

Cocktail Essentials

Some of the bars provide their own recipes for key ingredients which are presented below. Other elements may be familiar to bartenders but not necessarily to those of us who are less-experienced mixologists living in different countries around the world. Therefore, we have included some additional basic recipes for your convenience.

The Regent Berlin
Homemade Coffee Liqueur
provided by the hotel's mixologist

INGREDIENTS

1 handful	espresso beans
1 handful	coffee beans
5 oz | 40 g	sugar
1	vanilla pod
1 fifth | 0.75 L	vodka

METHOD

Crush the coffee and espresso beans in your hand and put in a 30 oz | 0.9 L container.

❖

Add the pulp of the vanilla pod and the sugar.

❖

Pour the full bottle of vodka over it, cover and steep it for four days.

The Greenwich Hotel
Homemade Spiced Grenadine
provided by the hotel's mixologist

INGREDIENTS

5 cups | 1.2 L	pomegranate juice
2 cups | 450 g	sugar
7 tbsp | 56 g	cardamom pods
3 tbsp | 24 g	cloves
4 tsp | 20 g	black peppercorn
2 tsp | 10 g	aleppo pepper*
1	vanilla bean, split and scraped
1 tsp | 5 g	sea salt

METHOD

Bring all to a boil and simmer 30-40 minutes.

❖

Strain and refrigerate immediately.

*The aleppo pepper, a variety of capsicum, is a spice primarily used in Middle Eastern and Mediterranean cooking. It has a medium heat and slightly sweet tang. Available in spice sections and online.

Cocktail Essentials

Chandler's at Cape Rey
Rosemary-Peppercorn-Beet Infused Vodka

provided by hotel's mixologist

INGREDIENTS

1 fifth | 0.75 L		vodka
	4	roasted beets with skin on, roughly chopped
	3	sprigs of rosemary
0.25 cup | 60 g		whole peppercorns

METHOD

Place all ingredients in an air-tight container and let sit for three days.

❖

Strain and enjoy!

Palazzo Avino
Alcoholate of Ginger and Fennel Seeds

provided by the Palazzo's mixologist

INGREDIENTS

2 tsp | 10 g fennel seeds
3.5 tbsp | 50 g fresh ginger
17 oz | 0.5 L vodka
17 oz | 0.5 L water

METHOD

Infuse the fennel seeds and fresh ginger in the vodka for 3 days.

❖

Filter out all ingredients and add the water.

❖

Let sit for several hours to meld the flavors.

Cocktail Essentials

Tenaya Lodge
High Sierra
Bloody Mary Mix
provided by the Lodge's mixologist

INGREDIENTS

1 qt | 1 L	Major Peters Bloody Mary Mix
1 tbsp | 15 g	celery salt
0.5 tbsp | 10 g	Kosher salt
2 tbsp | 30 ml	Tabasco
2 tbsp | 30 ml	Worcestershire sauce
2 tbsp | 30 ml	tapitillo hot sauce
0.5 tbsp | 10 g	wasabi powder*
1 tbsp | 15 g	fresh cracked pepper
2 tbsp | 30 g	raw horseradish
2 oz | 58 ml	fresh lime juice

METHOD

Mix all ingredients together.

❖

Best when left to sit for several hours.

❖

Hacienda Petac's
Jamaica (Hibiscus) Syrup
provided by the Hacienda's mixologist

INGREDIENTS

2 cups | 473 ml	hibiscus flowers
2 cups | 473 ml	water
1 cup | 236 ml	sugar or agave nectar

METHOD

Brew dried hibiscus flowers in water.

❖

Bring to a strong boil, remove from heat.

❖

Let steep for 20 minutes. Remove flowers.

❖

Bring to boil again and add sugar
or agave nectar.

Boil until reaching the consistency of syrup.

❖

Let cool and store in airtight container.

** Be sure to use authentic, not faux, wasabi.
Available in most stores and online.*

Cocktail Essentials

Velas Vallarta
Simple Syrup

Makes about 1.5 cups | 355 ml

Simple syrup is a popular ingredient frequently used in cocktails and other drinks. This recipe can be refrigerated in an airtight jar for up to 1 month.

INGREDIENTS

1 cup | 225 g	granulated sugar
1 cup | 237 ml	water

METHOD

In a medium saucepan, combine sugar and water.

❖

Bring to a boil, stirring, until sugar has dissolved.

❖

Allow to cool.

❖

Store in a sealed container.

Aqua Expeditions
Kampot Pepper Syrup

Makes 2 cups

INGREDIENTS

2.3 cups | 134 g	sugar
6	whole star anise, roughly chopped
6	vanilla beans, split in half
3 tbsp | 30 g	pink peppercorns

METHOD

Bring 8 cups of water and the sugar to a boil.

❖

Add anise, vanilla beans, peppercorns and boil 1 minute.

❖

Remove the star anise and vanilla beans from the syrup and divide them equally between jars.

❖

Ladle in hot syrup and peppercorns.

❖

Strain before using.

❖

Store unused portion in fridge.

Cocktail Essentials

Scrub Island
Peach Purée
Makes about 2 cups | 454 g

This simple recipe is for those who do not have their own and prefer fresh peach purée to jarred. It can be made the day before. Freeze leftovers in portions for future use in preparing peach margaritas, bellinis, salad dressings, desserts, and other recipes.

INGREDIENTS

- 3 whole large peaches
- water for boiling
- sugar to taste

METHOD

Bring a pot of water, enough to cover the peaches, to a boil.

❖

While the water heats, wash the peaches and cut a large X on the bottom of each one.

❖

Fill a bowl large enough to hold all the peaches with cold water and ice cubes.

❖

When the water reaches a boil, carefully lower each peach with a large spoon into the pot.

❖

Boil for 1-2 minutes until the peaches float and the skin starts to peel off.

❖

Immediately transfer them to the bowl with the ice water.

❖

Let the peaches remain in the ice water for 2-3 minutes and then drain.

❖

Carefully remove and discard the skins.

❖

Slice the peaches into large chunks. Discard the pits.

❖

Place the peach chunks in a food processor and mix until smooth and creamy. If the mixture is not sweet enough, add a little sugar to taste.

Pour the purée through a fine mesh strainer and into a clean jar. Discard any leftovers in the strainer.

Basic Bar Glassware

Olives for oil production, Umbria, Italy

Appetizer Essentials

Below are recipes for additional ingredients used in various appetizers. Many were submitted by the hotel, resort and cruise line chefs as part of their appetizers; others are versatile components for which you may or may not already have a favorite recipe.

The BodyHoliday
Tropical Fruit Chutney
Makes: 3 cups | 175 g

INGREDIENTS

0.25 cup | 60 ml	red wine vinegar
2 tbsp | 30 ml	light brown sugar
2 tbsp | 30 ml	honey
0.25 tsp | 1 g	ground coriander
1.5 cups | 265 g	finely diced pineapple, (0.5 in | 12.5 mm cubes)
1.5 cups | 265 g	finely diced mango, (0.5 in | 12.5 mm cubes)
1 cup | 175 g	finely diced papaya, (0.5 in | 12.5 mm cubes)
1	small garlic clove, minced
0.5 tsp | 2 g	finely grated fresh ginger
pinch	pinch ground cloves
1	cinnamon stick, 2 in | 50 mm
1	small bay leaf
1/2	small Scotch bonnet or habanero chile, minced
	salt and freshly ground white pepper to taste

METHOD

In a large saucepan, combine the vinegar, brown sugar, honey, cinnamon stick, cloves, coriander, and bay leaf.

❖

Bring to a simmer.

❖

Add the pineapple, mango, papaya, garlic, ginger and Scotch bonnet.

❖

Season to taste with salt and white pepper.

❖

Simmer over a low heat for 30 minutes. Let cool.

❖

Discard the cinnamon and bay leaf.

❖

Serve at room temperature or chilled.

Appetizer Essentials

El Conquistador Resort
Sofrito
Makes: 2 lbs | 1 kg

As the base for most Puerto Rican dishes, sofrito can be added to beans, rice, soups, stews -- almost anything. Homemade is preferable and seasoning can be varied to suit your taste.

INGREDIENTS

2 lbs | 1 kg	plum tomatoes
2	red bell peppers, seeded
2	medium yellow onions
5	garlic cloves, smashed and peeled
1 bunch	cilantro, large stems trimmed
0.5 cup | 118 ml	extra-virgin olive oil
1 tbsp | 15 g	salt
1 tbsp | 15 g	black pepper

METHOD

Coarsely chop the tomatoes, peppers, and onions.

❖

Add the garlic, cilantro, salt and pepper.

❖

Divide into batches and pulse in a food processor until finely minced.

❖

Heat the olive oil in a large pot over a medium heat until it glistens.

❖

Add mixture and cook for 25-30 minutes, stirring occasionally, until reduced and thickened. Do not let the mixture brown around the edge.

❖

Cool to room temperature. Store in an airtight container in the refrigerator for up to two weeks. Freeze in portions for up to six months.

Appetizer Essentials

The Oyster Box
Horseradish Mayo
Makes: 0.66 cup | 158 ml

INGREDIENTS

0.5 cup | 120 ml	mayonnaise
1 tbsp | 15 g	horseradish
2 tsp | 10 g	chopped fresh chives
2 tsp | 10 ml	fresh lemon juice
pinch	pepper

METHOD

Mix all ingredients.

❖

Cover and chill until ready to serve.

❖

Store in an airtight container in refrigerator up to 1 week.

South Seas Island Resort
Jerk Seasoning
Makes: 0.33 cup | 110 g

INGREDIENTS

1 tbsp | 15 g	garlic powder
2-3 tsp | 10-15 g	cayenne pepper
2 tsp | 10 g	onion powder
2 tsp | 10 g	dried thyme
2 tsp | 10 g	dried parsley
2 tsp | 10 g	sugar
2 tsp | 10 g	salt
1 tsp | 10 g	paprika
1 tsp | 10 g	ground allspice
0.5 tsp | 2.5 g	black pepper
0.5 tsp | 2.5 g	dried crushed red pepper
0.5 tsp | 2.5 g	ground nutmeg
0.25 tsp | 2.5 g	ground cinnamon

METHOD

Combine all ingredients and mix well.

Store in an airtight container for up to 3 months.

Appetizer Essentials

Palazzo Avino
Garlic Confit
Makes: 4 cups | 0.9 kg

For garlic lovers, garlic confit is no stranger. It's handy to keep in the fridge for pasta and other sauces, topping pizza, making garlic mashed potatoes, herb and guacamole dips and much more.

INGREDIENTS

3 cups | 0.7 kg	unpeeled garlic cloves *(about 100-125 cloves)*
3 cups | 0.7 L	extra virgin olive oil

METHOD

Fill a large bowl with cold water and a few ice cubes. Set aside.

❖

Bring 2 quarts | 1.9 L of water to a fast boil in a medium saucepan.

❖

Place the unpeeled garlic cloves in a sieve and dip them in the hot water for about 20 seconds to loosen the skins.

❖

Remove the sieve from the boiling water and dip in the ice water. When the cloves are cooled, place on a cutting surface, remove root ends and the skins should slip right off. Pat dry with clean paper towel.

❖

Place the peeled garlic cloves in a heavy, medium-sized saucepan. Add the oil, covering the cloves by 0.5 in | 13 mm.

❖

Heat the pan over a medium heat.

❖

As soon as it begins to bubble, reduce heat to the lowest setting on your stove. It should not exceed 220°F | 104°C. Use a mesh utensil to skim any skin fragments that might surface.

❖

Carefully cook the cloves for about 40-45 minutes, stirring occasionally to avoid browning. Once they are very tender and the garlic becomes a light golden color, remove the pan from heat and set aside. Allow the cloves to cool in the oil.

❖

Store in an airtight container and refrigerate for up to one week. Always bring the confit to room temperature before using, and use a clean spoon to remove the garlic.

APPETIZER ESSENTIALS

GRAND VELAS RIVIERA NAYARIT
SPICED BREAD CROUTONS

Makes: 6 cups | 1.4 kg

INGREDIENTS

0.5 cup	113 g	butter or margarine
6 cups	540 g	bread cubes, *approx. 8-10 bread slices (baguettes work well)*
0.5 tsp	0.25 g	basil
0.5 tsp	025 g	pepper
0.5 tsp	0.25 g	marjoram
0.5 tsp	0.25 g	oregano
0.5 tsp	0.25 g	thyme
0.5 tsp	0.25 g	dill weed
0.5 tsp	0.25 g	garlic powder
0.5 tsp	0.25 g	ground celery seed
		salt to taste

METHOD

Preheat oven to 350°F | 177°C.

❖

Melt butter/margarine.

❖

Add spices to butter/margarine and mix well.

❖

Pour mixture over bread pieces to coat.

❖

Spread bread evenly on cookie sheet.

❖

Bake for 10-15 minutes or until golden brown.

SOUTH SEAS ISLAND RESORT
CARIBBEAN SLAW

Serves: 4-6

INGREDIENTS

1/2		head green cabbage, shredded
1		red bell pepper, thinly sliced
1/2		red onion, thinly sliced
2		carrots, peeled and shredded
1		mango - peeled, seeded, and diced
0.5 cup	20 g	fresh cilantro, chopped
0.33 cup	85 g	nonfat plain yogurt
2 tbsp	30 ml	reduced-fat mayonnaise
1 tbsp	15 ml	prepared yellow mustard
1 tbsp	15 ml	apple cider vinegar
1 tsp	5 ml	agave nectar
		salt and black pepper to taste
1 dash		habanero hot sauce to taste

METHOD

In a large bowl, toss the cabbage, red bell pepper, red onion, carrots, mango, and cilantro.

❖

In a small bowl, whisk together the yogurt, mayonnaise, mustard, cider vinegar, agave nectar, salt, pepper, and hot sauce.

❖

Pour the dressing over the cabbage mixture and toss to coat.

❖

Put the slaw in the refrigerator and allow to marinate for for 1-2 hours to thoroughly blend the flavors.

Appetizer Essentials

South Seas Island Resort
Tostones
Makes: 12-14

Tostones are usually made of green plantains and served as appetizers with cocktails before dinner. They are also commonly found as accompaniments for fish, meat, or poultry dishes. Green plantains are used to make tostones and are fried twice. After the first frying, they need to be smashed to make chips, sliced or molded into cups which are called tostones rellenos. For these, you need a molding utensil called a tostonera which can be found in Latin markets or online. To make flat chips or slices, you can pound the fried plantains with a meat hammer or other similar or heavy device.

INGREDIENTS

2	large unripe green plantains
1 cup | 237 ml	olive or canola oil for frying

METHOD

Heat the oil in a small heavy skillet over medium heat.

❖

Cut plantains crosswise or at a slant into 1 inch | 25 mm thick pieces and remove all the peel.

❖

When oil is hot, put a few plantain slices at a time in the oil and cook for about 3 minutes until golden. Do not crowd the pan.

❖

Drain on paper towels.

❖

Repeat with the remaining slices.

❖

When all slices are cooked, flatten them to about a 0.25 inch |6 mm thickness.

❖

In a bowl of warm salted water, dip flattened plantains, 1 at a time, then drain them well on paper towels.

❖

Heat reserved oil over moderate heat until hot, but not smoking, and fry flattened plantains in batches, without crowding, for about 3 minutes until golden brown.

❖

Transfer to paper towels to drain.

Appetizer Essentials

Hacienda Petac
Corn Tortillas
Makes: 24

INGREDIENTS

2 cups | 256 g	masa *(corn tortilla mix - preferably Maseca brand)*
0.5 tsp | 2.5 g	kosher salt
	vegetable oil for brushing

METHOD

Whisk the masa and salt in a medium bowl.

❖

Stir in 1.5 cups | 375 ml of water

❖

Knead in bowl until dough forms. The dough should feel firm and springy and look slightly dry. Add more water by tablespoonfuls if too dry and crumbly or add a little more masa if too wet.

❖

Measure 1 heaping tbsp | 15 g dough and roll into a ball.

❖

Flatten on a tortilla press lined with a plastic bag. If it crumbles, add more water; if it sticks to the plastic, add more masa. Repeat pressing out remaining tortillas.

❖

Heat a large cast iron skillet over medium-high heat and lightly brush with oil.

❖

Cook 2-3 tortillas at a time for 1-2 minutes until charred in spots and the edges start to curl.

❖

Turn over to finish cooking — about 15 seconds.

❖

Transfer to a kitchen towel lined with paper towel and fold over to keep warm.

❖

Repeat in batches with the remaining dough.

APPETIZER ESSENTIALS

W Scottsdale
White Balsamic Vinaigrette
Makes: 1 cup | 237 ml

INGREDIENTS

0.66 cup | 156 ml	extra virgin olive oil
0.25 cup | 60 ml	white balsamic vinegar
1 tbsp | 15 ml	honey
1 tbsp | 15 ml	lemon juice (about one generous squeeze from a fresh lemon)
	kosher salt and freshly ground black pepper *to taste*

METHOD

Combine the vinegar and lemon juice in a bowl.

❖

Slowly whisk in the oil until fully combined.

❖

Whisk in the honey.

❖

Season to taste with salt and pepper.

❖

Let stand at room temperature for 30 minutes to let the flavors meld.

❖

Whisk dressing well just before serving.

Condado Plaza Hilton
Fried Plantains
Serves: 5-6

As plantains ripen, the color changes from green to yellow to black, much like the banana, and become sweeter. They are never to be eaten raw. For this recipe, only use the yellow.

INGREDIENTS

3	yellow plantains
	olive or canola oil for frying
	salt to taste

METHOD

With a sharp small knife, cut the ends from each plantain, then cut a lengthwise slit through skin.

❖

Cut plantains lengthwise into 1-inch-thick pieces.

❖

Beginning at slit, pry skin from pieces.

❖

In a deep fryer or large deep skillet heat 1.5 in | 4 cm of oil to 375°F | 190°C on a deep-fat thermometer

❖

Fry plantains in batches, without crowding, turning frequently until tender and just golden — about 2 to 3 minutes on each side.

❖

With tongs transfer plantains as fried to paper towels to drain.

❖

Best served immediately.

Cocktail Index

Metropolitan Locales

Agri Cola	41
Barrel-Aged Rendezvous	23
Beet Infused Rosemary Ginger Cocktail	51
Bitchin' Sangria	49
Bushman's Delight	35
City Lights	21
Espressotini	31
Fluffy Bunny Cocktail	43
Milestone Old Fashioned, The	25
Orient Express	39
Rubens Royal Blush	45
Smoking Red Rose, The	37
Thyme Sloes Down	33
Tropical Bliss	19
Veruschka Cocktail	27
Very Berry Spicy Margarita	29
Vitamin W Cocktail	47

In the Countryside

Gilded Age Cocktail	59
Greenbrier's Original Mint Julep, The	57
High Sierra Bloody Mary	65
Perfect Wharekauhau Gin Martini, The	61
Smashing Pumpkins	67
Sunlight Martini	55
Umhlanga Schling	63

In the Islands

Cabana Cocktail	75
Captiva Cooler	79
Caribbean Pink Passion	71
Laucala Lagoon	81
Lemon Rose Cocktail	85
Mojito Caribe Frozen	73
Scrub Island Flirt	77
Stairway to Heaven	83

South of the Border

Basil Martini	103
Coco Rumba	101
Cucumber & Habanero Chili Margarita	93
El Flamboyan	91
Sangria de Coco	89
Macho Margarita	97
Mango Caribe	95
Passion Fruit Dry Martini	99
Rhubarb Sour	105

Afloat

Kampot Fix	109
Zorro Dry Martini	111

Appetizer Index

Beet Chip Crudité with Curried Candied Pecan Dip	*157*
Bocadita de Res	*155*
Breaded Mussels Stuffed with Ricotta and Sausage	*123*
Bringing Back the "Vol-au-Vent"	*151*
Carpaccio and Ceviche of Mahi-Mahi	*133*
Coral Trout Ceviche	*131*
Curry Coconut Shrimp with Pineapple & Caramelized Leeks	*147*
Diver Scallops with Carnaroli Risotto (Dairy Free)	*145*
"Emiliano" Tuna with Avocado Aguachile	*117*
Esquites (Roasted Corn Dip)	*127*
Fruit Salad	*165*
King Lobster on Bread "Pizzaiola" Style	*141*
Lemon Grass Shrimp Skewers	*115*
Lobster Cocktail "Uniworld"	*163*
Locanda Verde's Crab Crostino	*125*
Maine Lobster Golden Citrus Salad	*159*
Pacific Bay Scallop Bruschetta	*129*
Pimm's Cured Salmon	*139*
Salad with Blackened Bluefin Tuna with Red Wine Sorbet	*161*
Salmorejo de Jueyes	*121*
Seafood Bruschetta	*143*
Seafood Taco	*135*
Shrimp Ceviche	*137*
South Seas Half Jerked Chicken	*153*
Spicy Calamari with Fresh Ginger	*149*
Tequila Grilled Shrimp Shooter	*119*

Index by Hotel/Resort/Cruise Line

Aqua Expeditions Aqua Mekong
Cambodia & Vietnam
Kampot Fix *109*

BBAR
London, England
Bushman's Delight *35*

Beau-Rivage Palace
Lausanne, Switzerland
City Lights *21*

Blantyre
Lenox, Massachusetts, USA
Gilded Age Cocktail *59*
Maine Lobster Golden Citrus Salad *159*

Body Holiday, The
St. Lucia, West Indies
Lemon Grass Shrimp Skewers *115*
Lemon Rose Cocktail *85*

Brown TLV Urban Hotel
Tel Aviv, Israel
Orient Express *39*

Bungalow, The
Santa Monica, California, USA
Bitchin' Sangria *49*

Casa Velas
Puerta Vallarta, Mexico
"Emiliano" Tuna with Avocado Aguachile *117*
Passion Fruit Dry Martini *99*

Index by Hotel/Resort/Cruise Line

Chandler's Bar & Lounge at Cape Rey
Carlsbad, California, USA
Beet Chip Crudité with Curried Candied Pecan Dip *157*
Beet Infused Rosemary Ginger Cocktail *51*

Condado Plaza Hilton
San Juan, Puerto Rico
Mojito Caribe Frozen *73*
Tequila Grilled Shrimp Shooter *119*

El Conquistador Resort & Las Casitas Village
Fajardo, Puerto Rico
Salmorejo de Jueyes *121*
Sangria de Coco *89*

Four Seasons Safari Lodge
Serengeti, Tanzania
Smashing Pumpkins *67*

Grand Velas Riviera Maya Playa del Carmen
Riviera Maya, Mexico
Breaded Mussels with Ricotta and Sausage *123*
Mango Caribe *95*

Grand Velas Riviera Nayarit
Nuevo Vallarta, Mexico
Basil Martini *103*
Salad with Blackened Bluefin Tuna and Red Wine Sorbet *161*

The Greenbrier Sulphur Springs,
West Virginia, USA
Greenbrier's Original Mint Julep, The *57*

Index by Hotel/Resort/Cruise Line

Greenwich Hotel, The
New York City, New York, USA
Agri Cola *41*
Locanda Verde's Crab Crostino *125*

Hacienda Petac
Merida, Yucatan, Mexico
Bocadita de Res *155*
El Flamboyan *91*

Hamanasi Adventure & Dive Resort Hopkins village
Stann Creek, Belize
Coco Rumba *101*

Hotel Casa 425
Ontario, California, USA
Esquites (Roasted Corn Dip) *127*
Very Berry Spicy Margarita *29*

Hotel Hassler Roma
Rome, Italy
Veruschka Cocktail *27*

Jade Mountain
St. Lucia, West Indies
Spicy Calamari with Fresh Ginger *147*
Stairway to Heaven *83*

Lafayette Hotel, The
San Diego, California, USA
Pacific Bay Scallop Bruschetta *129*
Smoking Red Rose, The *37*

Index by Hotel/Resort/Cruise Line

Laucala Island
Fiji
Coral Trout Ceviche *131*
Laucala Lagoon *81*

Hôtel Le Toiny
Saint-Barthélemy, French West Indies
Cabana Cocktail *75*
Carpaccio and Ceviche of Mahi-Mahi *133*

Matlali Hotel Punta de Mita
Nayarit, Mexico
Macho Margarita *97*
Shrimp Ceviche *137*

Milestone Hotel, The
London, England
Milestone Old Fashioned, The *25*

Montague on the Garden
London, England
Thyme Sloes Down *33*

The Oyster Box
Umhlanga, South Africa
Caribbean Pink Passion *71*
Pimm's Cured Salmon *139*

Palazzo Avino
Ravello, Italy
King Lobster on Bread "Pizzaiola" Style *141*
Sunlight Martini *55*

Index by Hotel/Resort/Cruise Line

QT Sydney
Sydney, Australia
Barrel-Aged Rendezvous *23*
Bringing Back the "Vol-au-Vent" *151*

Regent Berlin
Berlin, Germany
Espressotini *31*

Royal Blues Hotel
Deerfield Beach, Florida, USA
Diver Scallops with Carnaroli Risotto (Dairy Free) *145*
Fluffy Bunny Cocktail *43*

Rubens, The
London, England
Rubens Royal Blush *45*

Scrub Island Resort, Spa & Marina
Scrub Island, British Virgin Islands
Scrub Island Flirt *77*

Singular Patagonia, The
Puerto Bories, Chile
Rhubarb Sour *105*

South Seas Island Resort
Captiva, Florida, USA
Captiva Cooler *79*
South Seas Half Jerked Chicken *153*

Tenaya Lodge at Yosemite
Fish Camp, California, USA
High Sierra Bloody Mary *65*

Index by Hotel/Resort/Cruise Line

Toucan Hill
Mustique, Grenadine Islands, Caribbean
Caribbean Pink Passion *71*
Curry Coconut Shrimp with Pineapple and Caramelized Leeks *147*

Tower Club at Lebua
Bankgkok, Thailand
Seafood Taco *134*
Tropical Bliss *19*

Uniworld Boutique River Cruise Collection
Europe, Russia, Egypt, India, China, Vietnam, & Cambodia
Lobster Cocktail "Uniworld" *163*
Zorro Dry Martini *111*

Velas Vallarta
Puerto Vallarta, Mexico
Cucumber & Habanero Chili Margarita *93*
Seafood Bruschetta *143*

W Scottsdale Hotel
Scottsdale, Arizona, USA
Fruit Salad *165*
Vitamin W Cocktail *47*

Wharekauhau Lodge
Pallister Bay, New Zealand
Perfect Wharekauhau Gin Martini, The *61*

About the Author

Linda Lang is currently travel editor for *Southern California Life Magazine*, a premier national publication focusing upon the Southern California lifestyle. She is also proprietor of Linda Lang's Taste of Travel, a publishing firm focusing upon luxury travel worldwide.

For over three decades, she has stayed in the world's most luxurious hotels, dined in their fine restaurants, and watched the as the art of the cocktail has become a significant part of the travel experience. She has traveled the Orient Express from Istanbul to Paris, seen bird's-eye views of the French countryside from hot air balloons, walked the cobbled streets of medieval villages and avenues of the world's great cities, and cruised the most exotic riverways of Europe and seas aboard the finest ships.

As in FIVE STAR RECIPES *FROM* WORLD FAMOUS HOTELS & RESORTS— the award-winning* first volume in her Taste of Travel series published in 2014—she presented a sampling of some of the world's finest hotels and resorts and their recipes for the table starting with brunch, soups and salads to entrées and desserts. Current news about the latest gourmet events and luxury travel offerings are also found on www.LindaLangsTasteofTravel.com.

Linda has also authored two eBooks -- THE PARTY PLANNER and EASY PARTY RECIPES, both available on Amazon.com. The third volume in her Taste of Travel series is scheduled for release in October 2017.

*2014 Bronze Award Winner in the Best Travel Book or Guide Category by the North American Travel Journalists Association.

Made in the USA
Middletown, DE
08 June 2021